COMPARATIVE METROPOLITAN EMPLOYMENT COMPLEXES

New York, Chicago, Los Angeles, Houston, Atlanta

This study presents an integrated analysis of a wide range of industrial, occupational, demographic, attitudinal, geographic, transportation, and institutional factors in terms of their impacts on the operation of metropolitan employment complexes and on the employment of particular segments of the labor force. In an empirical and concrete approach, both common and distinctive elements of the five areas are identified and their significance for analysis and policy formulation is examined.

CONSERVATION OF HUMAN RESOURCES: 7

OTHER VOLUMES IN THE
Conservation of Human Resources Series

Comparative Metropolitan Employment Complexes

New York, Chicago, Los Angeles,
Houston, Atlanta

by **DALE L. HIESTAND** and **DEAN W. MORSE**

Foreword by Eli Ginzberg

LANDMARK STUDIES

Allanheld Osmun   MONTCLAIR
Universe Books   NEW YORK

ALLANHELD OSMUN AND CO. PUBLISHERS, INC.
19 Brunswick Road, Montclair, N.J. 07042

Published in the United States of America in 1979
by Allanheld, Osmun and Co. and by Universe Books
381 Park Avenue South, New York, N.Y. 10016
Distribution: Universe Books

LIBRARY OF CONGRESS CATALOGING IN PUBLICATION DATA

Hiestand, Dale L.
  Comparative metropolitan employment complexes.

  (Conservation of human resources series)
  "Landmark studies."
  1. Labor supply—United States—Case studies.
2. Metropolitan areas—United States—Case studies.
I. Morse, Dean, joint author. II. Title. III. Series.
HD5724.H37   331.1'1'0973   77-84456
ISBN 0-87663-822-1

The material in this publication was prepared under contracts 21-26-73-51,
21-36-75-20, 21-36-76-18, from the Employment and Training Administration,
U.S. Department of Labor, under the authority of Title III, Part B of the
Comprehensive Employment and Training Act of 1973. Researchers undertaking such projects under government sponsorship are encouraged to express
freely their professional judgment. Therefore, points of view and opinions
stated in this document do not necessarily represent the official position or
policy of the Department of Labor.
  Reproduction by the U.S. government in whole or in part is permitted
for any purpose.

Printed in the United States of America

Foreword

Some books are more difficult than others to place in context. In the scholarly realm, a work that asks new questions, that goes beyond established methodology, and that stops short of providing quantifiably testable results is difficult to describe and assess. The Hiestand and Morse study belongs in this category.

The new question that it addresses is whether it is possible and profitable to describe five of the nation's largest labor markets—those of New York, Chicago, Los Angeles, Houston, and Atlanta—with an aim of uncovering what they have in common as well as identifying the unique characteristics that differentiate them.

While earlier investigations have studied one or another metropolitan labor market, such as the Shultz and Rees study of Chicago, for the most part analysts have relied more on intensive than extensive approaches. They have selected one or two critical dimensions such as wage rates and commuting time from residence to work site in an effort to deepen understanding of the interaction between these two parameters on the allocation of labor among competing employers.

Hiestand and Morse have approached the problem differently. Their present thrust has been descriptive—to make explicit the range of different types of employment systems that exist within each of these metropolitan centers; followed by a comparative analysis among the five large centers; and, only at the end after the multiple structures and mechanisms have been described and gross comparisons and differences illuminated, do they focus on the more traditional questions of the allocation of available jobs among competing individuals and groups.

It may help the reader if I briefly outline what is implied by the author's use of such terms as structures and mechanisms, which together comprise the basic elements of an employment system.

Structures involve geographic barriers which often determine the limits to the area; the Hudson River in New York and Lake Michigan in Chicago are examples. The demographic composition of the population is clearly important with its varying proportions of minorities and types of minorities, some of whom may, and others of whom may not, be English-speaking. Then, there are the shaping influences reflecting the industrial structure; a city like Chicago with its heavy accent on producer and consumer durable manufacturing differs in important ways from a white-collar metropolis like New York or Atlanta with their heavy concentrations on trade and commerce.

Since it is characteristic of modern metropolitan life that people live shorter or longer distances from where they work, the transportation systems on which the several communities rely significantly influence their labor market operations. New York, with its extended subway system and interurban commuter trains, has the capacity of moving people daily between home and work at a volume, time, and dollar cost quite different from what is possible in Los Angeles with its overwhelming dependence on the freeway.

Among the important institutions and mechanisms that must be considered in any sophisticated analysis of a metropolitan labor market, the authors identify: (1) the availability of educational and training institutions, for access to them largely determines the initial skill preparation of new entrants into the labor force; (2) the extent to which trade unions have succeeded in organizing sectors of the labor market, with consequences for recruitment, assignment, wage levels, and productivity; (3) the way in which local political organizations deal with civil service and patronage in the rapidly growing public sector, particularly as they affect the distribution of opportunities for public employment among different groups in the community; and (4) the methods that employers use to recruit new workers, ranging from reliance on their own work force for referrals to long established relations with particular schools and training institutions.

It would be highly gratifying to report that the authors have in fact succeeded in each of their three assignments—that is, in describing the range of institutions and mechanisms that underlie what they call an "employment complex," in carrying out their gross comparative studies of the parallels and differences found among these complexes in the five metropolitan areas, and in providing a dynamic model for assessing the interaction patterns among the principal elements out of which these complexes are constructed. But, once one identifies the interacting elements that require assessment—which include the flows of persons in different demographic groups, both from within the area and from outside, and both into and out of the metropolitan labor market; the rate of the local economy's growth (or decline) and the corresponding job creation and job distribution in different sectors; the occupational shifts resulting from these general and specific growth trends; and shifts in various power centers, particularly in access of different groups to political patronage and to trade union membership—the difficulty in the undertaking becomes self-evident.

Hiestand and Morse have provided the reader with a broadened framework—concrete detail about each of the five metropolitan labor markets, and selected analysis (primarily in Chapter 5), where they seek to sort out what is common and what differs in these five centers as to patterns of employment for youth, for adults, and for different minority groups including women, blacks, and the Spanish-speaking population. The authors recognize that their study is exploratory. Their primary effort has been directed to demonstrating the need for a more inclusive and variegated framework to influence the range and diversity of conditions that charactertize the employment systems in these five metropolitan centers. Hence, Chapter 5, as well as the other chapters, are to be read as illustrative and suggestive, not as definitive.

This promising investigation has not been able to focus on many important questions, a few of which may be identified in order to suggest future directions for research.

How do the range and quality of the skills that are locally produced via the educational and training systems set a limit to the scale and direction of the expansion of a metropolitan center? Can shortfalls in the skill pool be compensated for by in-migration and to what extent?

If the economic base of a metropolitan center begins to erode, as did New York's during the 1970s, or levels off, as it appears to be doing in Los Angeles, is this a process that once begun is likely to feed on itself by encouraging the out-migration of the more skilled and talented young persons who will seek better opportunities elsewhere? And if they leave, does that simply reinforce the initial weakness and lead to a further erosion of the economic and employment base? What can slow, stop, and reverse such an unraveling process, once it gets under way?

Is it possible, by in-depth studies, to assess the differential opportunities and limitations that minority groups with varying characteristics face, such as the Spanish-speaking in Los Angeles and the black immigrants from the Caribbean in New York City? How does the analyst rack up the critical qualities characteristic of different minority groups and assess them within the context of differing economic and employment conditions in different metropolitan markets?

Much the same question can be asked about the differential barriers and opportunities that face the female worker. The authors also note the striking differences between Houston and New York in the expansion of employment in the public sector. Since we now know, on the basis of the experience of the mid-1970s, that New York was unable to maintain its much expanded public sector, is there any way, through the comparative study of large metropolitan labor markets, to develop bench marks that can be used to alert persons in policy-making roles when the danger point is being approached in the expansion of the public sector?

More broadly, might prospective comparative metropolitan labor market studies yield new insights about future occupational changes, migration patterns, labor force participation rates, and other key variables that would help to inform the leadership in the public and private sectors of the dangers and opportunities that lie ahead so they might seek constructive resolutions that would help strengthen each metropolis's economic and employment base?

These, and other questions that could be formulated, reinforce the earlier observation that the present study must be viewed as exploratory. The structures, institutions, and mechanisms that interact one with the other to draw people into the work arena and distribute them among competing employers have not been studied with sufficient care to support broad generalizations about the ways in which large metropolitan labor markets operate. But, if the effort by Hiestand and Morse whets the interests of other researchers to address this important, if relatively neglected, subject—three out of every ten working Americans are in metropolitan complexes at least as large as Atlanta—then this exploratory effort will have been justified.

Eli Ginzberg, Director
Conservation of Human Resources
Columbia University

Acknowledgments

We want to thank Eli Ginzberg and Alfred Eichner for their astute comments on the formulation of this study and Eli for his careful reading of the successive drafts. Students in a number of classes and seminars in the Graduate School of Business, Columbia University, made significant contributions to our thinking via their projects, term papers, and discussions. In the five metropolitan areas under study here, we received invaluable aid from innumerable experts and practitioners in local labor markets and employment systems; from analysts and officials of the United States Bureau of Labor Statistics, the Equal Employment Opportunity Commission, state employment divisions, municipal manpower agencies, and chambers of commerce; from university researchers; from local officers of the Urban League and the Recruitment and Training Program, Inc.; and from a wide range of personnel officers in manufacturing, retailing, financial, utility, service, civil service, and other enterprises. In particular, we want to thank former Secretary of Labor James D. Hodgson and K. R. Kiddoo of Lockheed Aircraft Corporation in Los Angeles; Samuel Bernstein and Dennis Mc Evoy of the Mayor's Committee on Manpower and Economic Development in Chicago; Earl Lewis of the Mayor's Office in Houston for arranging many of the above meetings for us.

We are also most grateful to Joseph Epstein, Chief, Division of Research Methods and Services, Employment and Training Administration, United States Department of Labor, for his careful reading of the final draft and his constructive comments.

We also want to thank Charles Brecher for smoothing the administrative way for our work, Sylvia Leef for arranging for typing and reproduction, Tom Wong for his cheerful and careful organization and computation of data, and Bernice Schuddekopf, Judy Dumas, Joan Henry, and others for their skillful typing. Finally, we want to thank our wives for adjusting their own academic, research, and vacation schedules to the exigencies of our research and writing schedules.

Dale L. Hiestand

Dean W. Morse

Contents

List of Tables and Maps

COMPARATIVE METROPOLITAN EMPLOYMENT COMPLEXES

CHAPTER

1

Introduction

This is a study of five complex metropolitan employment systems in and around New York City, Chicago, Los Angeles, Houston, and Atlanta. The primary purpose of the study is to develop and apply a conceptual scheme for the analysis of employment processes and patterns in the context of very large urban areas. The five metropolitan employment complexes provide a basis for exploring concretely the adequacy of the conceptual scheme.

This study explores the thesis that fundamental factors that shape employment patterns differ significantly among major metropolitan areas; that these differences have a major impact on the way each large metropolitan employment complex operates; and that these differences have a differential impact on the employment experiences and patterns of different groups in each metropolitan area. To the extent this is true, employment, manpower, and related programs and policies may have to be differentiated among large metropolitan areas if they are to be operationally effective.

This study is distinctive for a number of reasons. First of all, it focuses on employment in a few of the largest metropolitan areas of the country. Many studies of urban employment focus on a large number of cities and often omit the largest cities altogether; they are really studies of employment patterns in middle-sized cities, for middle-sized cities predominate in the computed averages. Secondly, this is a comparative study. Most studies of employment in the context of large cities or metropolitan areas focus on a single city or area with no explicit outside reference points. Thirdly, this study emphasizes distinctive differences, whereas most studies focus on what is common to, or the average, for all the cities in a study. Fourthly, this study is more comprehensive than most, dealing with and integrating many major aspects of each labor market. Most studies of urban employment deal with one or a few aspects of the labor market, such as variations in job-finding techniques, labor mobility, wage levels, or minority employment patterns.

More particularly, this study seeks (1) to identify major differences in the structure and/or institutions of metropolitan employment complexes and (2) to determine whether these differences produce significant differences in the way these employment complexes operate: with respect to how jobs and workers are found, with respect to mobility patterns, and with respect to the allocation of jobs among young people, minorities, and women.

This is an exploratory study. Employment in the largest metropolitan areas has not been adequately analyzed, in part because such areas are so complex. We cannot afford, however, to ignore the problems they present because the analysis cannot be easily structured. This study can therefore be seen as an attempt to develop typologies and analytical techniques to deal with large, heterogeneous employment systems. As such, conceptualization plays a major role, along with data analysis.

These issues have usually been discussed under the rubric of "urban labor markets," but we do not find that concept useful. The term "labor market" is frequently used loosely and has never been carefully conceptualized, particularly in a geographical context. In the first place, only certain aspects of employment take place in a market context: hiring, departure, and rehiring. Many aspects of employment take place within organizations or other structured systems. People tend to move from job to job and to be trained and promoted within enterprises or organizations. The concept of the "internal labor market" has been developed by Doeringer, Piore and others[1] to deal with this problem, but the key point is that large organizations function rather more as systematic employment allocation mechanisms than as markets. Indeed, when most large organizations deal with the labor market, i.e., when they hire or release personnel, their operations tend to be systematized. Moreover, certain kinds of employment and mobility, which take place in a market context as workers move among companies, are nevertheless highly structured. Among unionized construction workers, for instance, complicated sets of rules determine who is employed by what employers. Thus, employment in a metropolitan area takes place or exists in a complicated set of labor markets and employment systems. We will call the aggregate of these markets and systems in a metropolitan area its "employment complex." This subject will be explored at greater length in Chapter 2.

Significant differences in labor market structure and institutions, the impact these differences have on labor market operations, and their possible policy significance is explored here in the context of five metropolitan areas centering on New York City, Chicago, Los Angeles, Houston, and Atlanta. The reasons for their selection will be set forth later. It is pertinent to point out, however, that the metropolitan areas centering on New York, Chicago, and Los Angeles include nearly 14 percent of the nation's labor force, and the five areas include nearly 16 percent.

COMMONALTIES VS. DISTINCTIONS AMONG METROPOLISES

That ours is an urban society is self-evident. That individual and group behavior and institutions are profoundly affected by urban environments is a working hypothesis of a large portion of social investigation and analysis. In all this interest and concern, there is often a somewhat curious and yet perhaps understandable assumption that urban life is more or less similar wherever it occurs, and, indeed, wherever an individual is located within any particular urban setting. Yet this flies in the face of much of our day-to-day experience. The world and national traveler knows that he can identify most of the large cities he enters without being told where he is. Something in the air, in the architecture, in the faces of the people, in the nature of street noise and traffic patterns tells him whether he is in London or Paris, Rome or Madrid, New York or Los Angeles, Manhattan or Brooklyn. Cities *are* different and city dwellers differ between cities and within cities. This seems always to have been the case, perhaps even more so in the past than today. Sparta and Athens, Jerusalem and Alexandria, Florence and Siena; the past distinctions are obvious to the historian and the present differences are obvious to the visitor.

Our common experience tells us that cities differ, but our conceptions, our theory, and our policies often seem to assume a similarity. Indeed, our national programs often seem to seek to impose a common frame on them. Much of our past national urban and labor market policy has been a procrustean bed. One possible explanation for this may be that in urban analysis there has been a strong tendency to focus on the common elements or similarities. In this, urbanists have followed standard scientific practice; i.e., they have assumed that cities all belong to a class of social entities and have sought to define them (1) in terms of central tendencies or averages, and (2) in terms of relationships between common variables.

From some points of view, this approach has been fruitful for it is obvious that cities have certain things in common. The efforts to account for some of the differences take many forms; in some cases, cities are separately analyzed in terms of size groups, major function, age, and region. Yet, at any point in time, the classification of cities often seems arbitrary. In their classic analysis based on 1950 data, Duncan and Reiss classified cities along two scales: first, whether they were national, regional or subregional in scope, and secondly, whether they were oriented toward manufacturing or were a service center.[2] In a significant proportion of cases, it was not clear whether to classify a particular city as a manufacturing or service center and/or whether it was national, regional, or subregional in scope.

By 1970, Thomas Stanback developed a much more sophisticated set of classes of city: nodal, manufacturing, resort type, government-associated, medical/education, and mixed type.[3] In his analysis he also used a large number of size classes, three or nine, depending on the level of analysis.

In these and similar analyses, it was clear that the largest cities presented the greatest difficulty. If given a weight in keeping with their relative sizes, one or a few cities dominate a statistical analysis, making it hard to see whether the findings reflected a "class" or a particular city. On the other hand, if the largest cities are given equal weight with other small cities, the scientific validity of the findings is equally dubious. Small cities influence the findings out of all proportion to their real importance. The problem is intractable and leads to some curious results. Edwin Mills, in his analysis of changes in the rate of growth and geographical dispersion of population and employment in cities, excluded New York, Chicago, Los Angeles, and Washington, D.C. on the grounds that they were not representative.[4] New York and some other of the larger cities have been classified as "miscellaneous" at times, for they fit no single framework.[5] One can argue that large cities are not representative, but then neither are small cities.

The problem can be illustrated in this way. Cities can be classified by several obvious features: size; industrial, and, presumably, occupational character; demographic structure; growth trends; age; transportation technology; and governmental structure. In addition, each city occupies a unique geographical location, with a particular pattern of land, water, slopes, i.e., a particular geographical configuration. Each city has, based on its unique history, a unique set of industrial plants, office structures, residential structures, and other capital assets. Each city, again reflecting its history of in-migration, population growth, and out-migration, has its own unique population complement. Each city may also have a relatively unique quality to the nature of its social, political, industrial relations, and intergroup relationships. All of these are to varying extents determinants of the nature of its employment complex. Given these many variables, any attempt to isolate the influence of each of them requires a very large number of observations. Of course, many of the

NEW YORK SMSA

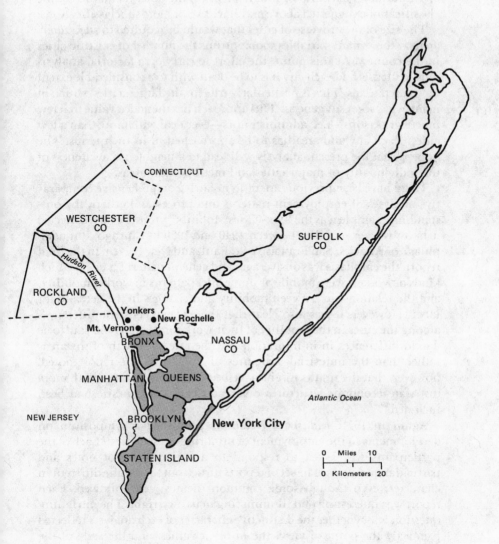

above variables may also be interrelated. On the other hand, each of the classifications suggested above may have two or more subclassifications.

The size of the universe of cities that would be required to adequately analyze these many variables soon outruns the number of existing cities in the country. At this point, the effort to carry on a factorial analysis must collapse, and each city has to be dealt with to a considerable extent on its own terms. This is particularly true for the largest cities, which in many ways seem sui generis. This approach has the added value that few practical persons—i.e., administrators—ever deal with more than a few cities. Each city and area has to be approached in its own terms. The hope is that the present analysis will lead to a heightened awareness of the individuality of major cities and metropolitan areas.

There have been previous attempts at fairly comprehensive comparative analyses of employment patterns and processes. Perhaps the outstanding example was the "Six-Cities Mobility" project which collected data on worker mobility between 1940 and 1950 in Chicago, Philadelphia, Los Angeles, San Francisco, St. Paul, and New Haven. In the final report, the emphasis was on averages and general patterns, i.e., on which kinds of workers were mobile or immobile, patterns in worker mobility, and the relationship between mobility and changes in the demand for labor. However, it was also clear that there were persistent differences among the cities in the mobility of their work forces. This was said to be due to differences in in-migration and the rate of growth of the areas rather than the industrial structures of the cities. The report noted, however, that the results might have been different "if cities with more disparate economic structures or greater variations in size had been included."[6]

Again in 1971, *Industrial Relations* published a symposium on developments in the employment of minorities in six cities.[7] Each of the participants was asked to respond to a common set of notes and particular questions. The set of reports turned out to be quite different in character, even though some common themes were followed. Each report was interesting and illuminating in its own right. The intriguing question was whether the distinctive character of each analysis reflected primarily the point of view, the implicit values, and the style of the several authors or, rather, primarily real distinctions among cities. This book, with each city being approached by the same analysts with the same explicit and implicit frame of reference, should help to provide an answer to that question.

More commonly, scholars have sought to understand the internal operations of particular city or urban labor markets by focusing on a single area. The Lloyd Reynolds study in New Haven,[8] the Hoover-Vernon study of New York City,[9] each attempted a degree of comprehensiveness, but the reference points were not clear. The Chicago labor

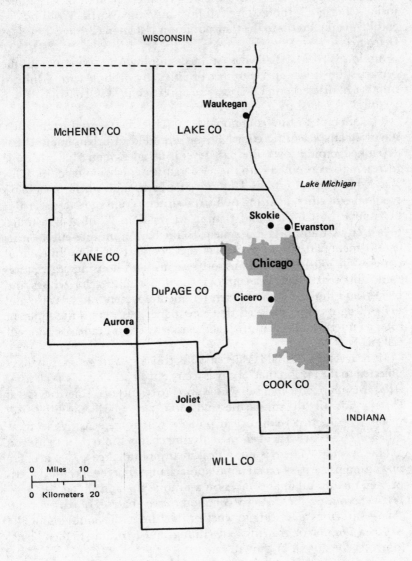

CHICAGO SMSA

WISCONSIN

McHENRY CO

LAKE CO

Waukegan

Lake Michigan

KANE CO

Skokie

Evanston

Chicago

DuPAGE CO

Cicero

Aurora

COOK CO

Joliet

INDIANA

WILL CO

0   Miles   10

0   Kilometers   20

market has been studied in unusual detail along a few axes: Albert Rees and George P. Shultz studied the geographical pattern of wage rates inside Chicago;[10] John Meyer, John Kain, and Martin Wohl related employment patterns to the transportation system in Chicago as well as Detroit.[11]

Again, Ray Marshall has studied employment patterns in the construction trades in a number of cities. By dealing with a limited number in discrete cities he began to approach the kind of study which we think is necessary.

The attempt to find commonalties in cities is essential in the early stages of any scientific effort. But as the field of urban analysis has developed rapidly over the past several decades, many have become increasingly concerned with the need to distinguish among cities. This was behind the efforts by Duncan, Stanback, and others to develop typologies of cities, utilizing industrial structure and size as criteria. But by comparing Chicago and Detroit, Meyer-Kain-Wohl demonstrated that a city's transportation system could have a unique effect on its employment patterns. In particular, they demonstrated how differential patterns in job location, transport systems, and housing segregation could differentially affect employment opportunities for whites and blacks, and thus produce differential unemployment rates. Walsh and his colleagues demonstrated that newspaper ads play quite different roles as intermediaries in the labor markets of San Francisco and Salt Lake City.[12]

More recently, Ronald Abler and his colleagues in geography have objected to the notion that "a city is a city is a city." Their *Comparative Atlas* uses maps and analyses with respect to twenty of "America's Great Cities to identify the similarities and, more particularly, the differences in order to help develop urban policies which are sensitive to these differences."[13] Karl Taeuber, in analyzing changes in residential segregation, asserts: "There is no typical metropolitan area . . . .There are prevailing patterns of racial population change, but the specific pattern in each metropolitan area takes on a unique size and shape."[14]

It is becoming increasingly common to see analyses of patterns and changes in cities according to whether they are in the South or not, the Northeast or not, or growing or declining, and according to their "age" (however measured) or growth rate.

THE METROPOLITAN AREAS SELECTED

As noted earlier, the metropolitan areas selected were those that center on New York City, Chicago, Los Angeles, Houston, and Atlanta. The first three were selected because they are the largest and the most complex. They include one in eight of all employed persons in the

LOS ANGELES SMSA

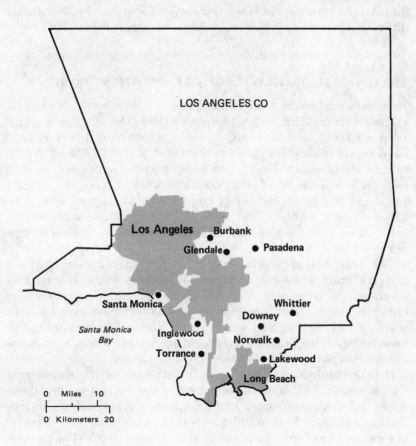

United States. These areas include a complex system of interarea, local and neighborhood labor markets, with significant regional, national and international dimensions. They warrant being analyzed in their overall complexity, for much of their character is suppressed when they are subsumed into analyses of particular aspects of urban labor markets.

The above three areas are located in the Northeast, Midwest, and West. Houston and Atlanta were selected to provide regional balance. They also permit an assessment of whether a style of analysis which focuses on differences is relevant and useful in areas that are considerably smaller than the primary trio.

THE GEOGRAPHICAL LIMITS OF AN EMPLOYMENT COMPLEX

How does one define a labor market or employment system in geographical terms? Although we speak of urban labor markets or of the labor market of particular cities, it has long been clear that every city's employment is inextricably intertwined with that of its suburban area. Much earlier research—and the tradition continues to date—focused on employment in central cities. Increasingly, however, it became critically important to analyze each city's employment along with that of its suburban area. Stanback and others, for example, have analyzed suburban labor markets both in their own right and in relation to their central cities.

The traditional approach therefore has been to analyze employment from the point of view of some central business district or city. This continues, in large part as metropolitan economies have expanded outward from historical agglomerations. As they have expanded, the shape of each agglomeration has been influenced by existing investments in buildings, factories, streets, utilities and residences, even as new investments have been made in all these categories.

Data on employment tend to come from two sources: the employer or the individual. The latter contains much more data on workers themselves and is generally more useful for labor market analysis. But the decennial census and monthly surveys of the labor force are collected at one's place of residence rather than at the place of work. Thus, census data moved early to the concept of metropolitan area. This had the effect of including within it many who worked in the central city but lived in outlying areas. It also had the effect of bringing into the data certain employed groups who have little or nothing to do with the major employment complex except in a peripheral or interdependent manner.

Thus, if one uses New York City as a reference point, the daily in- and out-flow of manpower extends to the east and northeast to Suffolk County and Connecticut, to the north and west to Putnam and Orange Counties, to the west almost to Pennsylvania, and to the south and

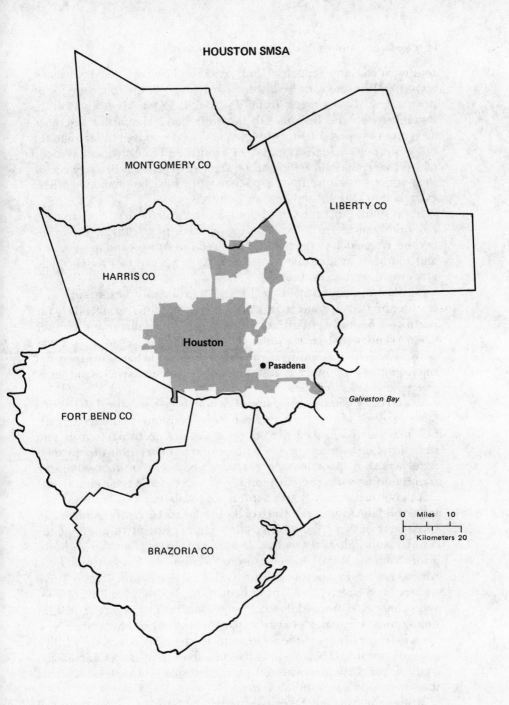

HOUSTON SMSA

MONTGOMERY CO

LIBERTY CO

HARRIS CO

Houston

● Pasadena

Galveston Bay

FORT BEND CO

BRAZORIA CO

0   Miles   10

0   Kilometers   20

southwest to Long Branch, Asbury Park, and beyond New Brunswick almost to Princeton. Indeed, some hardy individuals commute for at least a few days a week from Philadelphia, Washington, Boston, Poughkeepsie, and beyond. On the other hand, the farther one goes away from the nodal center of New York City or indeed of Manhattan, the more one includes population groups and employment systems which are primarily local in nature. Some enterprises in Brooklyn draw their entire work force from Brooklyn, while the labor market of others extends into Queens and Nassau County.

In a similar manner, it should be recognized that the Chicago economy and set of interrelated labor markets extends to the north beyond Winnetka, to the west at least as far as Aurora and to the south and southeast around the corner of Lake Michigan to East Chicago, Hammond, and Gary, Indiana.

Similarly, the Los Angeles region includes not only the geographically intermingled city and county of Los Angeles, but also extends to the northwest beyond Oxnard, to the southeast to Anaheim and Orange County, and perhaps to the west to Riverside and San Bernardino. These politically defined subunits of the state of California have all grown and intermingled economically into one great economic system and set of interrelated labor markets.

But do daily commuting patterns define the geographical limits of a labor market? This is perhaps a convenient notion, encouraged by the fact that our basic data are collected via the decennial census and thus focus on workers or would-be workers in relationship to their residences. But labor markets extend beyond and are more than the connection between presently employed persons and their employers.

A major metropolitan area's influence in labor market terms extends far beyond the zone of residence of those who are currently employed in it. Aspects of New York City's labor market extend throughout the country and indeed the world. It attracts lawyers from the Midwest, actors from the West, physicians from Pakistan, professors from South Africa, former businessmen from Cuba, laborers from Puerto Rico, waiters from Greece, cooks from Bengal, nurses from the Philippines, and seamstresses from Malaysia. Some come legally; others are illegal immigrants. Los Angeles attracts workers at various levels from New York City, the Midwest, the Southwest, Mexico, Japan, and the Philippines. Houston and Atlanta have had an active inflow from all across the country, but particularly from the rural and small town areas all across their states and surrounding states.

Most of these inflows take place at a relatively early age, say, at around age eighteen for laborers and clerical workers; age twenty-two or so for teachers and other college graduates; and age twenty-eight or so for professors or physicians. Others enter a new labor market at still later

ATLANTA SMSA

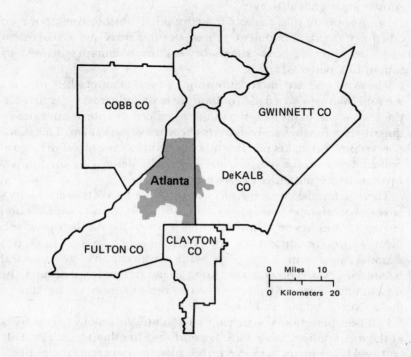

ages: the Oklahoman who sells his or her business at age forty-five to move to Los Angeles to start a new business; the physician who sells his or her practice in Chicago to accept a salaried position with a Houston hospital at age fifty-five or to establish a part-time practice in Phoenix; or the mid-level executive who is transferred into an Atlanta or New York corporate office at the age of forty. With each of these movers, there may also be a spouse making a similar entry into a new metropolitan labor market, sometimes as a partner or co-worker, but more often as an entirely independent worker.

On the obverse side, particular metropolitan areas lose manpower to other metropolitan, nonmetropolitan, or rural areas, and to that extent each metropolitan area extends beyond the boundaries defined by commuting patterns.

The extraordinary interrelationships of local labor markets within a metropolitan area on a daily commuting basis and across the entire continent or world in the case of relocations reflects, of course, our extraordinarily fast, flexible, and relatively cheap transport system. This transport system also makes possible other kinds of expansions of the metropolitan labor market beyond the boundaries defined by the journey between home and office or factory.

There is, for instance, a distinct seasonal shift. Part of the central city's labor force migrates seasonally to rural or resort areas to work for and among vacationers and those fortunate enough to take their jobs with them: writers, restauranteurs, beauty operators, etc. In some cases, this seasonal movement takes place within conventional geographical boundaries: New Yorkers to the Long Island shores. In other cases, the seasonal movement extends beyond the area or region: to the Adirondacks, New England, or Florida.

Fast transportation also means that a significant amount of the work of the metropolitan labor force is performed in other areas. The daily and weekly stream includes executives, advertising technicians, political personalities, truck drivers, stewardesses, and the like: New Yorkers to Washington, Chicago, and elsewhere, with similar streams in and out of the Chicago, Los Angeles, Houston, and Atlanta regions. The transport system plays a key role in the location of corporate offices, accounting firms, management consultants, etc. In this very concrete form, metropolitan employment systems increasingly extend beyond the conventional norms defined by the location of the primary job and of the primary residence.

The previous discussion makes clear that there is no totally satisfactory way to define the geographical boundaries of a labor market or a complex of employment systems. Employment systems tend to be focused on enterprises. For a variety of economic reasons, the enterprises in a metropolitan area tend to be more centrally located than are the residences. Most metropolitan areas have secondary employment centers, such as at airports or industrial complexes, but here too the residencies of the workers are more widespread than the places of employment. Some employment systems may exist at one location in a metropolitan area, but many extend over an area or several areas. Certain workers pursue careers within retail, service or banking chains which service all or major parts of a metropolitan area. However, executives, sales managers, civil service employees, and the like often move from one metropolitan area to another while remaining inside their particular employment systems.

For persons choosing jobs and employers seeking workers, the location of the job, the location of residences, and the linking transportation systems are all factors that shape the labor market. Some people tend to be fixed by the location of their residence; for them the labor market is shaped by those employers who are acceptable in a calculus involving both job and transportation possibilities. For most people living in the suburbs, jobs located in the central city are largely irrelevant. On the other hand, some people are primarily focused on the job, and their secondary choices involve both residential and transportation possibilities. The fact that a New York City executive lives in Connecticut does not necessarily make Connecticut a part of the New York City labor market. Rather, for many New York City based executives, Connecticut is seen or used as one of their housing-transportation options. Indeed, the fact that many headquarters have relocated to Connecticut in part to be near where their executives want to live, emphasizes its role as a housing market. Thus, executives living in Connecticut might include some who are not interested in a job outside of Connecticut, some who work in Connecticut but would be interested in New York opportunities, and some who work in New York but live in Connecticut as a matter of choice, while still others might work in Connecticut or New York but see their futures in terms of relocation in the United States or abroad.

This emphasizes even more the arbitrary nature of the boundaries utilized in the study of metropolitan employment complexes. At one time, we gave serious consideration to defining the five complexes to include entire metropolitan regions. We ultimately rejected this on several grounds: first, the addition of secondary metropolitan areas (such as the Newark, Jersey City or Stamford SMSAs* to the New York SMSA, or the Galveston SMSA to the Houston SMSA) would only further complicate an already complicated analysis. It would arbitrarily add to the distinctive character of each metropolitan employment complex, tending to bias an analysis focusing on distinctive aspects.

*Standard Metropolitan Statistical Area.

Moreover, closely adjacent metropolitan areas do not seem to be closely related in labor market terms, however close they may be geographically and how much they may be interrelated economically. For instance, Manhattan, the core of the New York SMSA, draws over 90 percent of its work force from within the SMSA and less than 9 percent from elsewhere (i.e., from all of New Jersey, Connecticut, parts of New York north of the SMSA, and the rest of the nation). Many in this 9 percent are critically important managers and professionals who may have in fact been recruited from the rest of the country or the world. As Table 1.1 indicates, in all five SMSAs, at least 90 percent of their work force live inside their respective boundaries; less than 10 percent live outside (indeed, only 3 percent for the Houston and the Chicago SMSAs). Most in-commutation occurs from just outside to just inside the perimeter of a metropolitan area, and is accompanied by a nearly equal amount of commutation in the other direction. Thus, there is commutation in both directions between the New York SMSA and neighboring SMSAs and counties in New Jersey, Connecticut, and New York; between the Chicago SMSA and neighboring SMSAs and counties in Indiana and Illinois; between Los Angeles County and SMSA and neighboring California counties and SMSAs; between the Houston SMSA and the neighboring Texas SMSA and counties; and between the Atlanta SMSA and neighboring Georgia nonmetropolitan counties.

Thirdly, the labor forces of the large city SMSAs are all very much larger than those of the other adjacent or interconnected SMSAs. In 1970, the New York City SMSA, which then included Nassau and Suffolk counties' 1.0 million, had a total labor force of 5.2 million, compared to less than 0.9 million in the Newark SMSA, and another 1.0 million in 6 other nearby SMSAs in New Jersey and Connecticut. The Los Angeles SMSA contained a labor force of 3.0 million, compared to a total of 1.1 million in the Anaheim, Riverside, and Oxnard SMSAs. The discrepancy is even greater in the Chicago and Houston regions, where the labor force of the major SMSA was roughly 10 times greater than that of the secondary SMSA (the Chicago SMSA with 3.0 million vs. the Gary-Hammond SMSA with 244,000; the Houston SMSA with 827,000 vs. the Galveston SMSA with 88,000).

For these reasons, the decision was made to restrict the analysis in this study to five major standard metropolitan areas. To repeat, that decision, while having much logic to support it, is in the end arbitrary. Employment markets never have precise boundaries, and political boundaries are largely irrelevant.

DIFFERENCES IN METROPOLITAN EMPLOYMENT COMPLEXES

The next chapter will indicate what we consider to be the present state of knowledge with respect to the factors which influence the nature of

Table 1.1   Residence of Persons Employed in Selected Parts of 5 SMSAs, 1970

Place of Work	Residence		
	Same as Place of Work	SMSA	Outside SMSA
Manhattan	28.2%	91.5%	8.5%
New York City	81.4	92.2	7.8
New York SMSA	93.2	93.2	6.8
Chicago	71.9	98.1	1.9
Cook County	90.5	97.9	2.1
Chicago SMSA	97.3	97.3	2.7
Los Angeles (City)	62.0	96.1	3.9
Los Angeles SMSA	92.8	92.8	7.2
Houston	75.9	97.6	2.4
Harris County	94.1	96.8	3.2
Houston SMSA	96.5	96.5	3.5
Atlanta	44.8	91.4	8.6
Fulton County	52.8	91.1	8.9
Atlanta SMSA	90.1	90.1	9.9

Source: U.S. Bureau of the Census.

urban labor markets in general, without reference to particular metropolitan employment complexes.

In the subsequent chapters, we will first identify significant differences among the selected metropolitan areas. The next step will be to assess the impact of these significant differences on the ways in which labor markets operate. Finally, we will ask what the implications of the operational differences are for manpower programs and policies.

It is almost impossible to distinguish cause from effect in a labor market, as in any social system. The interactions are so complex that nearly everything can be said to be both cause and effect, i.e., that there are complex vectors simultaneously acting on the system, with complex linkages through time. For purposes of analysis, however, it may be useful to try to identify proximate causes and proximate effects. For purposes of discussion, we can group the possible differences among metropolitan labor markets which act as proximate causes into three different classes: structural, formal institutions, and informal institutions. Later, we will group the proximate effects as labor market operations, processes, and results.

The structural factors tend to be tangible, physical, readily identified, or easily counted. They tend to be independent of the labor market factors; at least they seem to affect the labor market more than it affects them. Wilbur Thompson has said of cities, "Tell me your industry mix, and I'll tell you your fortune." In a very real sense, the industrial structures of a metropolitan area, their technologies, the grouping and location of the physical structures in which they are housed—all these define the occupational and many other features of an urban labor market. But the labor market may also be shaped by other relatively tangible, objective, or structural characteristics: the geographical configuration of the area; the demographic, educational, and social character of the existing population; existing housing patterns and districts; and the existing transportation system. All these structural factors are relatively long-lived; they are imbedded in capital assets or people. While they may be initially influenced by the labor market, that influence is rarely predominant. Once they are in existence, moreover, they become part of the environment within which the employment complex operates.

The second class of factors by which major metropolitan areas may significantly differ may be described as the formal institutions which are part of or closely related to employment systems. Among these are collective bargaining agreements; laws regulating employment, licensing, etc.; seniority and promotion systems; recruitment, informational and placement systems; educational and training institutions and programs; and alternatives to employment, such as welfare programs and pensions. Many of these formal institutions have been consciously established to regulate or organize employment and the labor market.

Finally, employment complexes may be influenced by a variety of informal or latent institutional forces, which may vary greatly from city to city. There appear to be significant differences among cities in the quality or tone of industrial relations, racial and ethnic group relations, attitudes towards women, the political system, and the role of employer and business groups in the community. Such intangibles often cannot be clearly described since they take no formal shape. But they do seem to differ from city to city, and, more importantly, may have a variety of impacts on the way in which employment systems operate.

DIFFERENCES IN LABOR MARKET OPERATIONS, PROCESSES, AND RESULTS

As noted earlier, we will focus on three different aspects of the operations of labor markets which may be affected by distinctive differences in their structure and institutions. The first aspect has to do with ways in which workers and employers are brought together. In the literature, these have been considered the operations in the external labor market, in contrast to internal labor markets which operate within large organizations and systems. Specifically, the question here is whether the previously identified differences in the structure and institutions of major cities significantly affect the ways in which employers seek and/or find workers, and the ways in which workers seek and/or find employment.

Methods of locating workers and/or employment are a function in part of the industrial and occupational structure of a city and its related areas. Also, the precise geographical features of a city and area, the location of its employment and residential centers, and the nature of its transportation system have a direct effect on the number and types of workers which might be available to particular employers and on the types of employment opportunities which might reasonably be considered by particular workers. Again, the particular demographic structure of the city, and especially the size and character of the local cohort entering the labor force for the first time, the number and types of new entrants from elsewhere, and the number and character of others seeking work will determine in part how employers seek out workers, and vice versa. Finally, the ways in which workers and jobs are sought will reflect the precise mix of formal intermediaries (schools and colleges, employment and placement agencies, trade unions, manpower programs, equal opportunity employment programs, etc.) as well as informal institutional forces (sex, ethnic and racial groupings and attitudes, the industrial relations style of particular, important employers, and the role of political groups in employment). For instance, job-finding techniques in the public sector in a particular city will depend in part on whether its political structure supports "merit" or "patronage" systems.

The second aspect of the operation of labor markets which may be expected to differ significantly from one metropolitan area to another because of its distinctive structure and institutions would be the processes of mobility. For the purposes of this study, this inquiry will be confined to the occupational mobility of individuals as distinct from intergenerational mobility. Mobility can take place via either external or internal labor markets. Mobility may be very much conditioned by the industrial structure of an area, particularly to the extent that particular industries have characteristic occupational structures, progression systems, training systems, opportunities for movement among related firms, and the like. However, similar firms and organizations located in different metropolitan areas may have different structures, systems, and practices with respect to the organization of work and hence the character of upward mobility opportunities and patterns. Again, mobility patterns may vary among metropolitan areas because of significant differences in overall growth rates in particular subsectors, or because of significant differences in opportunities for outside study and training, in industrial relations and trade union practices, or in promotion practices.

The allocation of jobs among different groups in the local population is the third aspect of labor market operations, processes, or results likely to be affected by a significant difference in an area's structure or institutions which will be examined here. In particular, we want to know whether and how previously identified distinctions among metropolitan areas affect the allocation of particular types of jobs between men and women and between majority and minority groups, defined racially or ethnically.

To repeat, we are not trying to encompass the entire workings of these major metropolitan employment complexes. We are focusing on the major distinctive differences among them. We are asking three sequential questions:

(1) Do the selected employment complexes have significant differences in their underlying structure and institutions?

(2) Do these differences make for significant differences in the way in which workers and jobs are sought, in mobility patterns, and in the allocation of jobs among different population groups?

(3) What are the implications of any identified differences among cities and related regions in labor market structure, institutions, and results for manpower programs and policies?

RESEARCH TECHNIQUES

With such a complex subject we have relied upon a synthesis of existing materials, interviews of persons with informed judgments, and original analysis of the United States Census and other data.

In identifying the distinctive structural and institutional characteristics of each metropolitan area, we have carefully examined existing studies and analyses prepared by specialists in each area. We have also carried on a lengthy series of discussions with persons who are considered most informed about labor markets in each area: academics, employment service specialists, trade union officials, employer and placement specialists, government officials and the like. Out of these discussions, analyses, and observations, distinctive structural and institutional features for each SMSA have been identified.

Finally, data on employment patterns, drawn primarily from the reports of decennial census, have been analyzed in detail to identify the effects of structural and institutional factors.

Based on this analysis, we present two concluding chapters. The first of these develops a reconceptualization of the essential factors to be considered in the analysis of any large metropolitan employment complex. The second identifies areas of interest for the future in the light of emerging economic, social, and political developments, and considers the implications of the whole study for future manpower and labor market programs and policies.

NOTES

1. Peter B. Doeringer and Michael J. Piore, *The Internal Labor Market* (Lexington: D. C. Heath, 1971).

2. Otis Dudley Duncan et al., *Metropolis and Region* (Baltimore: The Johns Hopkins University Press, Resources for the Future, 1960).

3. Thomas Stanback, Jr. and Richard V. Knight, *The Metropolitan Economy* (New York: Columbia University Press, 1970), pp. 128-31.

4. Edwin S. Mills, *Studies in the Structure of the Urban Economy* (Baltimore: The Johns Hopkins University Press, Resources for the Future, 1972), pp. 26-27, 40-41.

5. See, for instance, Juan de Torres, *Economic Dimensions of Major Metropolitan Areas: Population, Housing, Employment, and Income,* National Industrial Conference Board, Technical Paper no. 18 (New York, 1968), pp. 5-9.

6. Gladys L. Palmer, *Labor Mobility in Six Cities: A Report on the Survey of Patterns and Factors in Labor Mobility, 1940-50* (New York: Social Science Research Council, 1958), p. 54.

7. "A Symposium: Equal Employment Opportunity: Comparative Community Experience," *Industrial Relations: A Journal of Economy and Society,* vol. 9, no. 3 (May 1970), pp. 277-355.

8. Lloyd G. Reynolds, *The Structure of Labor Markets: Wages and Labor Mobility in Theory and Practice* (New York: Harper, 1951).

9. Edgar M. Hoover and Raymond Vernon, *Anatomy of a Metropolis* (Cambridge: Harvard University Press, 1959).

10. Albert Rees and George P. Schultz, *Workers and Wages in an Urban Labor Market* (Chicago: University of Chicago Press, 1970).

11. John Meyer, John Kain, and Martin Wohl, *The Urban Transportation Problem* (Cambridge: Harvard University Press, 1965).

12. Marion Johnson and John Walsh, *Help Wanted: Case Studies of Classified Ads* (Salt Lake City: Olympus, 1976).

13. Ronald Abler, ed., *A Comparative Atlas of America's Great Cities: Twenty Metropolitan Regions* (Minneapolis: University of Minnesota Press, 1976).

14. Karl E. Taeuber, "Racial Segregation: The Persisting Dilemma," *The Annals of the American Academy of Political and Social Science,* vol. 442 (November 1975), p. 89.

Types of Employment Systems

INTRODUCTION

The focus of this chapter will be on the characteristics of particular types of employment systems which may exist in metropolitan employment complexes and may make for differences among them. We utilize the terms "employment systems" and "employment complexes" rather than "labor markets." The latter term has come to have specialized meanings which we do not think are as useful or insightful as they might be when comparisons are to be made between those basic processes which take place in large metropolitan areas which have to do with the recruitment of various types of labor and the subsequent mobility patterns which determine how workers will fare over their work-life.

To point up the contrast between our approach to the subject and the conventional approach to labor markets, it will be helpful to outline in summary fashion what is generally meant by the term "the labor market," when it is used by labor market theorists. Classifying labor markets as a sub-type of markets in general, economists have usually begun their analysis with the assumption that labor markets, like markets in general, are more or less competitive in character. In other words, a large number of buyers of labor services (employers) confront a large number of sellers of labor services (job seekers) in a market situation. Employers and job seekers are free to enter or leave the labor market. In this competitive model of the labor market, the price of labor services (the wage rate) tends to bring the quantity of labor services offered into equality with the quantity demanded.

The demand for labor is derived from the demand for the product which it helps to produce. The supply curve of labor has traditionally been taken to be related to the marginal disutility of work (or the value of leisure), but recent labor market theorists have increasingly emphasized the importance of alternative costs and opportunities. For example, women enter the labor market when they perceive that the value of their market wage exceeds the value of their nonmarket activities. Young people similarly balance the value of additional educational investment against income foregone.

The model of the competitive labor market therefore asserts that labor market behavior is fundamentally rational and maximizing in character. Moreover the individual worker is taken to be generally well-informed about the alternatives that face him, although it is also recognized that the acquisition of information about these alternatives is in itself a costly procedure. As a result, a worker's search for employment is viewed as a search for information about wage dispersal, the job searcher continuing to search only so long as he considers that the value of additional search is greater than its cost.

Labor market theorists recognize that in principle there exist as many labor markets as there are distinct types of labor (obviously a very large number), but they also emphasize that it is often quite easy to substitute one kind of labor for another. Conceptually, therefore, the boundaries between different labor markets are delineated by these substitution possibilities (technically, by elasticities of substitution). It should be noted in this respect that the movement of a worker from one labor market to another is considered to be a matter of free and informed choice, determined entirely by the worker's perception of the benefits and costs associated with the prospective move. Labor market theorists have always paid considerable attention to the price of different types of labor. In addition to the general wage rate (a shadowy concept at best) wage rate differentials by occupation and industry have been in the forefront of their concerns. Since wage rates for what appears to be the same kind of labor can vary geographically and indeed between firms located near each other, wage dispersal has also received increasing emphasis in their theoretical formulations and empirical investigations. What distinguishes present day labor theorists from earlier ones is a preoccupation with investment in human capital or the increases in income over lifetime due to such factors as education, on-the-job training and experience, investments in health, and geographical relocation. In effect, labor has been dissected into what are considered natural ability and capacities acquired through education, training, and the like. Much of the compensation for what appears to be labor alone is, in reality, a return to capital invested in human beings.

Even though much attention is given to education and training, the focus of labor market theorists still remains strongly fixed upon the actual transactions that take place in labor markets. Among these focal points are such events as hirings, quits, and dismissals, along with entries into and withdrawals from the labor force itself. Unemployment is related to those factors which determine the optimal length of job searches, along with the pattern of dismissals and quits, entries, and withdrawals. The ultimate focal point, however, is the determination of the wage rate for particular types of labor and therefore the determination of the quantity of employment through the interaction of demand and supply schedules. Flows into and out of particular labor markets are, in this conceptual framework, primarily determined by the pattern of wage rates and the technical possibilities of substitution of different types of labor between different labor markets.

Although labor market theorists are in some instances concerned with nontechnological barriers between subsets of the labor market (for example discriminatory practices), they are usually rather narrowly interested in how such barriers are related to wage rate differentials. For example, discrimination is often identified by differences in wage rates which do not reflect differences in the productivity of workers. If differences in wage rates can be satisfactorily accounted for by differences in such factors as educational attainment, training, and experience, then it is concluded that no employment discrimination is taking place, no matter how much discriminatory educational practices may have affected educational attainments or how much discriminatory barriers to entry may have affected training and experience attainments.

In other words, employers and employees are simply following the rules of maximization of profit on the one hand and maximization of utility on the other. In this view, the competitive labor market will, in fact, always tend to eliminate wage differentials unrelated to productivity differentials, except where employers have a "taste" for discrimination or are rationally responding to pressures of other interests (for example, unions) which have a similar "taste." Even when employers with a "taste" for discrimination discriminate more than others, it is concluded that those firms which discriminate least will grow larger and in this way, as Kenneth Arrow puts it, competition will tend to lessen discrimination and "only the least discriminating firms survive." Arrow's reservations about the applicability of the competitive model to the real world is indicated by his concluding remark. "Since in fact racial discrimination has survived for a long time, we must assume that the model . . .must have some limitation."[1]

It should be emphasized that the primary structure of the competitive labor market is provided by the institution of the market itself. Although each actor in the market is assumed to act in and for himself, the market is nevertheless an integrated system. The firm is considered to be a single, undifferentiated actor (the familiar black box) personified by the term, "the employer." Similarly a worker is viewed in an atomistic fashion, and he is active in the labor market only when he is actually engaged in a labor market transaction. During the times he is actually employed, he is no longer considered to be in the job market, although of course he is in the labor force.

The nature of the supply of and demand for labor is sometimes not clearly defined when the operation of the labor market is under discussion. One solution is to assume that workers and employers are, in principle at least, continually recontracting from day to day, so that all employees are part of the supply and demand curves of the labor market, even though only a small fraction are actively engaged in what are usually considered to be labor market transactions. In this formulation, all those who are employed at a point of time are in the labor market, exchanging their labor services for income. The structure of wages and the distribution of manpower, in this view, are all aspects of the labor market equilibrium at a point in time.

Another solution is to consider that the labor market per se is made up only of flows of vacancies and job seekers. In this case, labor market transactions represent the matching of job vacancies and job seekers, and the analysis centers upon how these matches are brought about. Since the matching process always involves a search process on both sides of the labor market, there will always be jobs waiting to be filled and job seekers searching for jobs.

The theory of competitive markets maintains that individual markets should clear themselves, prices changing until excess demand or excess supply disappear. It is therefore something of a problem to the labor theorists, who assume that labor markets are fundamentally competitive in character, that there should be instances of persistent unemployment. Imperfections of the labor market are considered among the most important (if not the only) causes of such persistent unemployment— imperfect information, the necessity of acquiring information through job search, artificial interferences in the working of the labor market (through such things as minimum wage legislation or trade union actions), these and the like are called upon to explain departures of the labor markets found in the real world from the norms of the competitive labor market model found in textbooks.

The imperfections that some economic theorists allude to in order to explain some apparent aberrations of the competitive labor market are considered by other labor market specialists to be the very essence of labor markets. Clark Kerr, representing one viewpoint, has emphasized the "balkanization" of the labor market, its manifold segmentation. Others, led by John Dunlop, have called attention to the paramount importance of "internal labor markets," highly structured by union-management operational agreements about recruitment, promotion, and dismissal procedures.

What are usually termed particular labor markets in any large metropolitan area might better be called employment systems. These systems produce ordered behavior over time and are given specific structure by a number of quite dissimilar elements. Institutions, mechanisms, and operations coalesce to lend an idiosyncratic character and structure to particular employment systems. Moreover, these structures are inevitably dynamic in character.

These particular employment systems, using our concept in place of the more restrictive concept of labor markets, are of great variety, ranging all the way from employment systems in which job transactions are concluded under quite competitive market conditions to employment systems in which the employment relationship between employer and employee is not the outcome of a transaction which, by any stretch of the mind, can be said to arise under competitive market conditions. As we have earlier stated, when we refer to the sum of the employment systems in a metropolitan area, we call the amalgam of employment systems the metropolitan employment complex.

This complex consists of the following fundamental types of employment systems:

1)   employment systems which depend on competitive labor markets
2)   employment systems which recruit for a limited number of entry positions and depend almost exclusively on internal promotion and transfers for other positions
3)   employment systems which rely heavily on internal systems, but with recruitment from the outside and/or departures to the outside at a significant number of points in the system
4)   systems which are structured via external agencies such as trade unions, professional societies, or licensing arrangements which control or strongly influence induction and interfirm mobility

There is no reason why the employment system and the related structure of a particular type of labor market, let us say one for construction workers, should be the same in different metropolitan areas. In fact, there is every reason why construction workers should be in employment systems which differ markedly in widely separated areas at different stages in their growth, with different governmental systems, confronting different geographical, institutional, and technological features, among many other factors. For example, at one extreme might be a system highly controlled by a business agent who favors his friends and supporters; at the other might be a hiring hall utilizing comprehensive computerized information and strictly defined procedures to allocate workers according to precise formulae. Employer associations, unions, and government may have collaborated to set up and run such a system.

This in essence describes the New York employment systems for some construction crafts. It can be understood only in terms of the specific history, character, and path of development of the local construction industry. The operation of these systems in turn depends to a high degree upon the present rates of growth of the region, upon the responses these employment systems make to the changing demography of the region, and upon the impact of new technologies upon the particular crafts and upon the location of construction activity and its character within the metropolitan region as a whole. Each metropolitan region has developed its own kinds of employment systems. For example, the type of construction activity (whether commercial, industrial, public, or residential), the location of construction activities in relation to other kinds of employment and in relation to residential patterns, the patterns of seasonality—all combine to give the various segments of the construction industry in each metropolitan region a somewhat different cast.

Examples, however, do not provide us with a schema for classifying and analyzing employment relationships and employment systems which may vary in important and precise character from one metropolitan labor market to another. To that task we now turn.

A TYPOLOGY OF EMPLOYMENT RELATIONSHIPS

We make frequent use of the term "employment relationship" in our discussion of employment systems. The employment relationship is at the heart of employment systems, but it is not the only relationship (or linkage) that makes up the complete configuration of employment systems. Contrary to transactions in the job market proper which are *events* and therefore take place at a moment of time (even if the job search and the recruitment process have been time-consuming), an employment relationship implies at least some time duration. Moreover, the relationship is dynamic in character. The mere passage of time tends to transform the relationship by altering the expectations and character of the two actors in the relationship, the employing agency and the employee.

Employment relationships do, however, range from the relatively transitory to the stable. Our typology of employment relationships is therefore based in part upon the temporal character of the relationship. The relationship can also be categorized by the kind of market structure and other institutional structures which encompass it. In addition, the relationship may also depend primarily upon the relative size and power of the two actors who form the relationship. Finally, the character of employment relationships is very closely related to the nature of the career patterns which emerge out of specific employment relationships.

For many years, a major facet of the work of a number of our colleagues in the Conservation of Human Resources, Columbia University, has been the delineation of career patterns. This effort has, among other things, entailed an analysis of the employment relationships which lie behind different types of career patterns. In their view, the critical element in the employment relationship is the degree and nature of the affiliation between the two parties, employer and employee. Although actual employment relationships are myriad, they can for many purposes be reduced to four basic types or combinations and variants of these types.

Eli Ginzberg has spelled out the nature of these four basic employment relationships as follows:

1) *Individualistic*—The individual is largely responsible for determining the conditions of his work.

2) *Organizational*—The individual holds a position in an organization which largely determines the work he does and the reward he earns.

3) *Market*—The individual's employment is continuous, but its terms are set by conditions of supply and demand in the labor market.

4) *Peripheral*—Here, too, the conditions of work are set by the market, but there is no continuity of employment. . .the individual is loosely attached to the labor force.[2]

It will readily be seen that the market and peripheral employment relationships emerge for the most part from labor markets which are near or at the competitive end of the spectrum of labor markets. The organizational employment relationship implies a considerable degree of institutional structure to the employment relationship, whether furnished by the employing unit or by employer organizations, or by governmental action. The individualistic group contains self-employed professionals, an assortment of independent small-scale businessmen, and persons of some degree of special talent and skill, like commercial artists and cabinet-makers. The individualistic group is characterized by a direct relationship with the purchasers of the services or goods they produce. Their customers are their employers, but they themselves control to a very considerable extent how and when they work. As Ginzberg puts it:

The dominant career pattern in our contemporary society culminates in an organizational relationship. This provides most men and women with basic employment security, reasonable income, and opportunities for advancement.

To exercise significant control over one's work (the individualistic relationship) requires either professional education, a specialized talent or skill, or the ability and willingness to take risks involving the potential loss of one's life's savings.[3]

For a significant portion of those individuals whose employment relationship is formally of the individualistic type, it is nevertheless true that some kind of organizational affiliation or tie to other institutions is strategically important. For example, professional societies or, among physicians, affiliations to hospitals, may give structure to what otherwise appears to be an atomistic relationship between the professional and his client.

The typology of the four major employment relationships provides us with a beginning schema by which to examine employment patterns in particular metropolitan areas, in order to disentangle common, unique, or unusually heavy concentrations of particular types of employment relations in these areas. At a later point, we can ask whether these patterns are in turn related to different ways in which the labor market and employment processes work in specific labor markets. We can also ask how strategic intermediaries and developmental institutions within a particular metropolitan area interact to produce particular patterns of employment relationships. In particular, we can address ourselves to the question of how different kinds of employment relationships are distributed among the major demographic groups that compose a particular metropolitan area.

The central questions with which this investigation is concerned are whether, how, why, and to what extent the five metropolitan areas differ in the ways in which two flows, the manpower flow and the flow of job opportunities, take shape and merge in the form of particular employment relationships and employment systems.

We have indicated that the boundaries between different employment systems are never impermeable. The same is true with the boundaries between the different types of employment relationships. How individuals move back and forth from one kind of employment relationship to another is critically important in the development of career patterns and in the opening up of options for those demographic groups whose options have been heretofore limited by patterns of discrimination or institutional barriers.

For those labor market specialists to whom has been delegated the task of developing policies and implementing programs to improve the equity and efficiency of particular metropolitan labor markets, a clear-cut sense of the specific features which make for the uniqueness of their own metropolitan region and the commonalties which it shares with other large metropolitan regions would seem to be a necessary foundation for appropriate policies, plans, and programs.

A TYPOLOGY OF EMPLOYMENT SYSTEMS

Employment systems, as noted earlier, are made up of a complex of relationships—between employer and employee, between employees and employees, between both employers and employees and a number of intermediary institutions. In general, such relationships involve processes that lead to more or less lasting affiliations, which in turn are developmental in character.

Two critical processes stand out. The first of these processes involves the institutions, mechanisms, and operations that lead to entry into a more than casual employment relationship. It centers around what Marcia Freedman has termed "the process of work establishment." The second process involves the institutions, mechanisms, and operations that shape the career pattern of workers in different firms, industries, and occupations.

One type of employment system has already been sketched. The competitive labor market is a relatively simple employment system where most of the structure is provided by institutional rules of the market itself (the legal framework primarily), which is characterized by short-term labor contracts, freedom of entry and exit, absence of linkages between participants (no unions or trade associations), and ample information. The formal requirements before a labor market can be termed "competitive" are so strict that only a limited number can be subsumed under that heading. Most involve relatively small firms, with high turnover of firms and workers, relatively low skill levels for the workers, relatively low levels of capital intensity and technology, and relatively flat organizational profiles. In large metropolitan areas, examples of relatively competitive labor markets exist, but it seems clear that in most metropolitan areas they do not play a predominant role in the totality of employment systems.

Nevertheless, there may be significant variation in the relative importance of the competitive employment relationship between large metropolitan labor markets. Small firms, found for example in some of the nondurable light manufacturing industries, often are characterized by relatively unstructured labor markets. Similarly, small firms producing services (for example, coin laundries, car washes, and small restaurants) often operate in competitive labor markets. Such firms, typically, make much more use of want ads and employment services than do firms whose employment relationships are structured by strong institutional rules and practices, formal and informal.

New York seems to have a relatively high proportion of firms with competitive employment relationships. Nevertheless, some nondurable light manufacturing and service industries in New York, which might be expected to have competitive labor markets, have in fact developed highly structured employment systems through employee organizations and trade associations interaction. These same industries often have a component, outside the structured part of the industry, in which competitive labor markets are predominant.

Similarly, some large establishments have what can be called a two-tier employment system, one part of which is highly structured, the other quite competitive. Some large financial institutions and insurance companies, for example, employ large numbers of women and minorities to perform the routine work associated with immense flows of paper. Such clerical personnel may in fact be hired in quite competitive markets, and the employment relationship between the establishment and the employee may approach what we have labeled competitive. Where unions are weak or absent and labor turnover at these occupational levels is high, the competitive market element is strongest. Again, New York appears to have a somewhat higher proportion of such establishments.

In addition, an important line of demarcation lies between blue-collar and white-collar employment systems. Even within a single firm, the employment systems for blue-collar workers may be expected to differ in systematic ways from the employment systems for white-collar workers. Recruitment practices, training and promotion systems, seniority and job security policies, grievance procedures, relations between superiors and subordinates, work rules and retirement practices—all of these important elements of employment systems usually differ between the "shop" and the "front office." Particularly important are the differences found in recruitment procedures. In some cases, a firm may be primarily blue-collar or primarily white-collar in character, e.g., a foundry in contrast to an insurance company. In such cases, the tone of the employment system of the entire company may be dominated by the primary importance of either the blue-collar work force or the white-collar work force.[4]

The level of technological sophistication also has a major effect upon the employment system of a firm. Technology determines skill levels, the importance of experience, the nature of work teams and the character of supervision. It in effect powerfully affects recruitment patterns, training and promotion processes, and other aspects of the employment system. In particular, high and rapidly changing technology is generally associated with those large firms which can or must maintain large research and development establishments and also have access to the large amounts of capital usually associated with high technology. Exceptions to this pattern exist, of course, but the correlation between high technology and capital-intensive operations is quite strong. The high levels of skill, dependability, experience, capacity to absorb further training, ability to move upwards along a long promotion ladder and to work harmoniously with others—all these factors make it necessary for high technology firms to recruit and hold onto a labor force, part of which must have unusual qualities of education, experience and character.

When a firm invests in the capital equipment in which high technology is embedded, it must, in order to protect the investment, simultaneously invest large sums in the recruitment and training of the work groups which are to man this equipment. Orderly and highly attractive career ladders are an important means of inducing members of the firm's labor force to expect to stay with the firm over long periods of time. Other inducements are also held out in the form of fringe benefits. Intensive efforts are made to induce workers to identify themselves with the firm.

Skilled workers who are able to operate new high technologies which are spreading rapidly to other firms and other areas are potentially mobile. All of the above elements combine to produce employment systems which are at the opposite extreme from the employment systems to be found in firms which utilize simple technologies which are often old and obsolescent. Nevertheless, adventurous and highly skilled persons often "spin off" from high technology firms to set up smaller service, research, consulting, and similar firms. In doing so, they often recruit added personnel from the larger firms, and, in the process, highly individualistic and market-oriented employment systems develop as a complement to the highly organized employment systems of the major employers.[5]

In industries characterized by low-level technology, capital intensity is usually low and equipment is often old and fully amortized. In these industries skills necessary to operate the equipment are widespread and relatively easily acquired. Many light manufacturing industries exemplify such cases. The employment systems found in this cluster of industries are to a large extent an expression of the nature of the technological level of the industries and the requirements that this technology imposes in the way of recruitment, training, supervision, and promotion.

Technology, however, is not the sole determinant of the employment systems of these light manufacturing industries. In fact, the technology is itself a reflection of the special character of these industries' production processes and of the individual firm's relations to one another and to auxiliary firms. In some industries it would technically be possible to devise a highly capital-intensive production process in which a number of elements of high technology could be utilized, but short production runs appropriate to a constantly shifting and therefore very uncertain production horizon make such capital-intensive equipment too unwieldy and therefore too risky. Firms must be able to expand and contract rapidly, or cease operations entirely for a while, or even go out of business as painlessly as possible. A number of years ago, A. G. Hart pointed out the consequences of this kind of uncertainty upon the willingness and ability of the firm to invest in fixed capital. It has the same kind of effect upon investment in the firm's work force.

Little investment in training a work force can be made by the typical firm in such industries and even less commitment to the production worker. Commitments which develop between workers and firms do so as a result of patterns set in negotiations between trade unions and employer associations. However, there may be firms and workers which are not covered by collective bargaining agreements. As a result, two parallel employment systems may exist within the same industry and metropolitan area, with some flow between the two. One system provides some degree of continuity and protection to the employee and a degree of predictability to the firm. The other is almost unstructured, and is in fact essentially a competitive labor market. Characteristically the latter employment systems rely to some extent upon recent immigrants to the area, including those from surrounding rural areas and illegal immigrants where they are available.

The capital intensity of a firm (the obverse of labor intensity) is also clearly related to the employment system appropriate to the firm. When a firm is highly capital-intensive, at the very least it must be able to place a high degree of trust in the stability, sense of responsibility, and competence of the workers who operate the capital equipment. While highly developed equipment does not always require high degrees of education or skill (a classical case of disparity between the level of technology and the technical competence of the worker is the high school graduate who is a member of a work group operating a nuclear reactor), very costly machinery invariably requires a high degree of dependability on the part of the operators. Often the very size and complexity of the capital equipment requires a coordinated work group, each member of which must be highly integrated with the rest of the group. Again, predictability and an elaborate drill requiring training and experience are sometimes necessary. A large jet liner is a model of such a work group. Some of the work is not in its nature highly skilled, but all of the work is tightly coordinated and must be performed by crews that are well-integrated and mutually self-policing.

Therefore, the employment systems of highly capital-intensive firms are often geared to create effective work teams, whether the teams are to be found in mid-air over the Atlantic or in front of a basic oxygen furnace in a Chicago steel plant. Continuity of operations and dependability of the work team is of the essence. Again, as in the case of high technology, it is worthwhile to the firm to make large investments in the creation of its work force and to offer considerable inducements to employees to stay with the firm. Recruitment procedures, training programs, promotion patterns, authority relationships—all will be affected to some degree by the overriding necessity of creating and maintaining a coordinated labor force which can, over time, be expected to maintain the levels of skill and experience necessary to maintain the continuity of operations characteristic of highly capital-intensitve industries.

We have already called attention to the importance of firm size in determining the characteristic of employment systems. Metropolitan areas do differ in terms of the distribution of firms by number of employees and therefore in the overall nature of their employment complexes. In part this is simply the inevitable result of competitive industries being necessarily composed of a large number of firms, each of which is relatively small and none of which can be expected to have a well-structured internal labor market. Perforce, a small firm cannot afford to maintain a differentiated personnel function, but at the same time it does not need such a bureaucratized employment system. Instead, its employment system, along with its employment relationships, will tend to be personal, idiosyncratic, and highly flexible. Since the employer himself has direct knowledge of the qualifications and character of employees (or can readily secure such information), credentials and formal screening and promotion procedures are not required. Training of the work force, if required at all, will be informal, direct, and on the job. If the small firm provides high level services or utilizes advanced technology in its production processes, it will be keyed into information and influence networks (e.g. as in the advertising industry) which will provide it with a qualified and easily expandable or contractable work force. Small, but advanced, laboratories, for example, may have close personal connections with local, regional, and even national institutions of higher education.

Large firms, on the other hand, must approach problems of manpower intake, training and development, promotion, and retirement in increasingly formal, predictable, and institutionally highly structured fashion. To the extent that the firm is a bureaucratic organization, all transactions that have to do with personnel tend to be based, in principle at least, upon merit and the attainment of formal qualifications, even if nothing more than a specified number of years in grade. Formal procedures may be bent and even broken in practice, but large firms tend to act as if they were universally applied and carefully conceal the exceptions. Even the top executives in such firms may be unaware of the extent to which private and hidden networks of influence and information modify the operation of the formal employment system. Outside observers, particularly if they are seen as threats to the existence of the informal employment system, will usually find it almost impossible to ascertain the actual state of affairs. It should not be assumed, however, that large firms invariably have similar employment systems. Marcia Freedman's *The Process of Work Establishment*[6] vividly illustrates the differences in the character and operation of the employment systems of three large firms in New York City, two of them large department stores, the other a large public utility. The firms differed in particular with respect to their recruitment practices, but promotion patterns and procedures were also markedly different, even between the two department stores. Wages, however, did not differ greatly.

What are some of the factors that may lead to such observed differences in the employment systems of large firms? Several immediately come to mind. First of all, the number of skill levels and the number of levels of control and administration can be expected to have an important influence upon the character of the firm's employment system. Where skill levels are few, promotion ladders are necessarily truncated. In terms of formal table of organization, the firm may be said to be relatively flat. On the other hand, the complexity of organization of a firm may require a number of levels of control. An orderly and formal progression from one level to another may be an objective of the firm's employment system insofar as its managerial staff is concerned. Similar considerations may apply to the technical staff if the firm's research and development activities are large and complex.

Whether a firm is local, regional, or national in scope obviously can have an important bearing upon its employment systems, particularly for managerial and technical staffs. National and regional firms ordinarily meet many of their needs for managers and technical staffs in particular metropolitan areas by relocating present employees rather than recruiting from outside the organization. Whether relocating existing personnel is characteristic of national and regional firms depends in part on the degree of centralization and therefore the size and character of its central headquarters. Relocation patterns may also differ for general managers, sales personnel, and research and development administrators and staff in the national or regional firms. Large metropolitan areas differ in the relative importance of national and regional firms. This is a reflection of the different positions large metropolitan areas occupy in the hierarchies of firms. Large metropolitan areas also differ in the willingness of high level personnel to accept transfers into them, depending on their amenities, climates, relative living costs, and the like.

The work process itself influences the employment systems of large firms. Whether the process involves continuous flows, large batches, or discrete units worked on by individuals at single work stations determine the degree to which workers belong to teams which must provide continuity of effort to the work process. When the work process involves a large-scale assembly line, for example in automobile manufacturing, the employment system of the firm must be able to absorb the impact of frequent and irregular absenteeism. The firm may have to develop a pool of part-time or part-week workers to supplement the nominally full-time, full-week work force.

On the other hand, a firm may specialize in the production of extremely large, costly, and complex products, like a major piece of defense or space hardware. If so, the firm's production force may work intensively for the period of the contract, but be subject to abrupt layoff if new contracts are not forthcoming. Both for individuals working in such firms and for the firms themselves, it is vital to develop employment systems which permit the rapid mobilization and shifting of high level technical and managerial personnel along with highly skilled production workers, while at the same time making tolerable the rapid contraction of the work force which occasionally takes place. The development of an extensive grapevine of information about, and contacts between, related firms is a common solution, both for the individual employee and for the firm.

Perhaps even more important than short-run stability or fluctuation is whether the firms or industries in a metropolitan area are growing or declining. Where growth has occurred and is confidently expected, employment systems must be geared to recruiting and upgrading of the work force. Linkages must be established with local, regional, or national education and training institutions, information and influence networks, and employment agencies, depending upon the size of the firm and the type of personnel required for expansion. A relative openness to new sources of qualified or qualifiable workers will be in order. Firms seeking to attract highly qualified personnel will have to offer relatively favorable career options and rapid promotion possibilities. At the same time, because they are operating in expanding and therefore profitable markets, these firms will usually be able to offer relatively attractive employment terms. Innovations in training and promotion practices may also be the result of a firm's response to the challenge of expanding and upgrading its work force. The Polaroid Corporation in Cambridge, Massachusetts, for example, has established procedures for low-skilled (and relatively uneducated) workers to move into technical positions, reflecting the conviction of its president that highly motivated workers can make much larger jumps, without formal education, than has been the practice in most United States industry.

Firms facing a decline in their work forces must develop quite different strategies for their employment systems. They must primarily be concerned with maintaining the morale and quality of their work forces in spite of declining opportunities for promotion and radically restricted, if not curtailed, recruitment. Guarantees that decreases in employment will take the form of attrition are one form of response. It is clear, moreover, that firms will try to ration carefully whatever openings do occur, either for promotion or at entry levels. Thus, declining firms and declining metropolitan areas tend to have characteristic employment systems and processes.

It is clear that employment systems are to a large extent the outcome of the particular market situation in which employing institutions and employees meet each other. In this respect, important elements of employment relationships and employment systems which evolve from these relationships will be determined by whether the employing institutions are private profit-seeking firms, nonprofit institutions, or government agencies. Hospitals, for instance, may be either private profit-seeking, private nonprofit, or public, and each type tends to have a somewhat different set of employment systems. Even so, there also may be different kinds of employment systems in, say, different government agencies.

Specific employment systems are the outcome of a large number of factors. It may prove useful to summarize at this point those factors which seem to be strategic. Our ordering of these factors is not intended to suggest a ranking of their importance, and it is evident that many of these factors are highly interrelated.

We called attention first to the importance of the size of the employing institution. Often related to the size of firm is the degree of capital intensity. Whether an employing institution is made up of primarily blue-collar workers, white-collar workers, or a mixture of the two is another critical determinant of employment systems. But the nature of these employment systems for both blue-collar and white-collar workers is also very strongly influenced by whether or not the firm's technology is highly advanced.

Important characteristics of the firm, insofar as they affect employment systems, are such things as the degree of unionization, the extent to which the firm relies upon groups of workers which constitute teams, the complexity of organizational structure, levels of skill and authority, and degree of centralization. Another important influence is whether or not the firm is primarily local, regional, or national in character. In particular, this affects how the firm's employment system relates to managerial and technical personnel.

Finally, employment systems are to an important degree affected by whether or not a firm, an industry, or an area is characterized by fluctuating or stable output levels, and whether or not the firm, the industry (and along with it the area in which it is located) is enjoying steady and significant growth or is trying to cope with a decline in employment opportunities. Firms, industries, and areas which lie between these two extremes can be expected to develop employment systems which differ in systematic ways from those which are found in situations of growth or decline.

We have discussed some of the factors that can be expected to impinge upon employment systems. The very multiplicity of such factors insures that a great diversity in the kinds of employment systems will be found within any large metropolitan area. Our discussion of these factors may have given the impression that employment systems in practice primarily center upon individual firms and their work forces. This is not always the case. The basic employment system in particular industries and occupations may be industry-wide or occupation-wide.

Industries in which hiring halls are found are prime examples of industry-wide local employment systems. But, there are a number of highly specialized and high-level service industries where the flows of individuals between relatively small firms is so continuous and so important a determinant of career patterns that it is necessary to focus upon the local industry rather than upon individual firms in order to understand recruitment, training, and promotion processes. The ancillary or intermediary institutions which affect how such industry-wide employment systems function range from the influence and information networks via professional schools to the personal ties between top level executive recruitment and placement agencies and the firms making up the industry. Management consultant firms also often play an important role in such employment systems.

It should be clear that our use of the term "employment systems" in contrast to the term "labor markets" is designed to emphasize our concerns with processes and operations that are broader than those usually subsumed under the heading, "the labor market."

The employment system includes all the formal and informal, manifest and latent institutions associated with the processes of recruitment, promotion, and termination of employment relationships in a particular firm, a particular industry, or a particular occupation. Although a job transaction is always part of an employment relationship, it can be, in fact, a relatively unimportant or automatic element in the totality of processes and operations that are involved in the entire employment relationship. Emphasis upon the employment system, moreover, precludes viewing either the job-seeker or the employer as atomistic and autonomous actors. On the contrary, they are linked to numerous agencies and institutions, constrained by mechanisms and institutions of which they are sometimes aware and sometimes more or less unconscious.

Complexity and diversity are the hallmarks of large employment systems. In Chapter 1, we indicated some of the structural features of large metropolitan areas that might be expected to influence the character of their employment systems in general. Many of these structural features act, from the point of view of existing employment systems, both as cause and effect. From some points of view, the structural characteristics of an area are simply part of the given to which individual employment systems in the metropolitan area must adjust in one way or another. From other points of view, structural features are themselves in part the results of kinds of employment systems that have emerged in the area over time. For example, the industrial and occupational composition of a metropolitan area is in part a function of the way its employment systems, either individually or collectively, have operated over long periods of time.

SEGMENTATION OF THE METROPOLITAN
EMPLOYMENT COMPLEX

Though expressions such as "the labor market" or "the urban labor market" are often encountered, they often do violence to the reality of large metropolitan employment complexes. There is no such thing as a general labor market for a metropolitan area. There are only specific labor markets.

Boundaries between these specific labor markets serve to give general structure to the total employment complex of a metropolitan area or region. One line of demarcation between labor markets is the simple one of geographical area. This kind of differentiation of the labor markets of a metropolitan area is always to be found. But the geographic configuration (physiognomy) and the transportation system of a metropolitan area may reinforce the geographical differentiation of its employment systems or tend to lessen its significance. The pattern and extent of geographical segmentation of labor markets can therefore be expected to differ in quite unique ways when very large metropolitan areas are being compared.

Moreover, once a geographical pattern of sublabor markets has developed in an area, it tends to persist over time because it has become embedded in the capital structure of the area, including its housing stock, its infrastructure, and its plant and equipment. Of particular significance is the spatial relationship, especially in older metropolitan areas, between residential areas, specific sublabor markets, and the mass transportation systems. Where, as in New York and Chicago, an important part of the mass transportation system takes the form of highly developed and extremely costly subway and elevated rapid transit lines, transporting (and needing to transport if they are to survive economically) vast numbers of workers to a relatively confined central business district, residential and job location choices are relatively constrained for a large portion of the region's work force and employers.

A second line of demarcation is the differentiation of labor markets within an area by occupation. The higher the level of skill, education, and experience required in an occupation, the more clear it is which workers and employers are in that market. Where skill levels are low and experience relatively unimportant, the distinction between nominally separate occupations may be nebulous and the market may be porous. For example, although the census enumerates a large number of separate occupations for operatives and service workers, many of these occupations are easily entered (and as easily left). The demarcation between occupations, particularly the higher skilled occupations, are quite frequently reinforced by a complex web of institutional arrangements and practices—for example, licensing and employment agency practices.

A major institution, which often contributes to the segmentation of employment systems, is the trade union. In attempting to secure better employment terms for its members, unions frequently take stringent steps to limit membership. Whether directly, through control of apprenticeship programs or the operation of hiring halls, or indirectly, because influence and information networks are open primarily to members, unions help to create and maintain highly structured, specific labor markets and employment systems and, in the process, limit access to particular employment systems to favored groups. Even so, the most important factor differentiating occupations of high levels of skill and training is the nontransferability of most of the skills developed in these occupations. The critical boundaries around such occupations are those that limit opportunities to education and training.

Another line of demarcation between labor markets within an area is by industry. If the training, for example, that an individual has received on-the-job or formally is specific to a particular industry, he or she can expect to gain the maximum return on this investment only by staying within that industry. In addition, a worker may have a considerable psychic investment in personal or group relationships with the specific types of people found primarily within a particular industry. He or she may initially have become affiliated to the industry or firm because the life-styles of co-workers were compatible and familiar. This is particularly true when the production process is based upon small and intimate working teams. Not only may individual workers find it difficult to part from the group; the group may find it even harder to absorb new members, particularly if the life-styles of new members are quite different.

It is, moreover, characteristic of some industries that they have become historically associated with particular ethnic groups (or, more likely, with a specific social stratum within an ethnic group). Ethnicity and industrial attachment varies greatly between and within metropolitan regions. In older metropolitan areas which experienced large inflows of immigrants in the early years of the twentieth century or, more recently, large inflows of Southerners, black and white, and Hispanics, the linkages developed between particular ethnic groups and particular industries and occupations differ markedly among metropolitan areas.

It should be apparent that the segmented labor markets already distinguished here do not necessarily constitute discrete universes. A particular worker will often find himself or herself confronting a number of lines of segmentation whose combined effect may be cumulative.[7] Taken together, these boundaries may locate him or her in a very small subsegment of the area's employment systems. For example, a secretary may be a member of a tightly knit work group of a nonprofit hospital, which in turn is part of a quite localized hospital complex. At the same time, she or he usually has a wide range of alternative opportunities as a secretary in either hospital-related activities or universities, governmental units, and private employers. The extent to which such multiple lines of segmentation restrict or expand the range of options open to particular individuals has been little explored.

A number of other factors, mostly social or institutional in character, contribute to the segmentation of a metropolitan area's employment systems into a number of specific labor markets. One of the most striking kinds of segmentation, broad in scope and deep in its effects, are those by sex. Segregation by sex or race (or by any other characteristic which is not uniquely related to productivity) is, from the point of view of economists, generally considered to be nonrational behavior. Nonrational or not, it is a pervasive element in the economy.

Moreover, patterns of segregation are, if not rational from an economic point of view, clearly the product of belief and value systems. In a country as large and diverse as the United States, in a system of cities whose histories, cultures, and social arrangements differ as much as the major metropolitan areas of the country do, it is to be expected that considerable variation in the specific patterns of discriminatory behavior by sex or race and in the intensity of such discrimination will be found between the large metropolitan areas.

Segmented labor markets extend from what are in fact highly competitive labor markets, in which all the workers may come from a particular ethnic group, sex, or race, to the opposite extreme of labor markets in which access is tightly controlled by complex webs of institutional, political, social, and value systems. One feature of the employment systems of large metropolitan areas is the great diversity of specific labor markets and employment systems to be found within them. It is one of the working hypotheses of this study that, along with the diversity to be found in all five of the metropolitan areas we have examined, there also exist patterns of labor market segmentation which are unique to each of the metropolitan areas.

A SUMMARY STATEMENT

The choice of a conceptual framework by means of which problems in the real world will be examined and analyzed; policies to remedy perceived defects in the operation of institutions developed; and programs designed to give effect to policies set up, implemented, and evaluated is so critical, and often so little appreciated, that investigators who have chosen different conceptual frameworks to analyze what seems to be a common subject often appear to be talking about entirely different matters.

A broader conceptual framework—particularly one which includes institutions on the periphery of labor markets and employment systems and which focuses upon processes which work themselves out over long periods of time—will, in our opinion, frequently identify and illuminate pervasive and profound institutional structures and patterns which do, in fact, discriminate severely against some demographic groups by restricting access to favored employment systems. In many cases, these institutional structures, patterns, and the resulting operations are entirely impersonal, automatic, and collective in their outcomes.

Our conceptual framework is therefore deliberately chosen to emphasize institutional structures and their social and economic outcomes. One stage upon which these institutions play their role is in the great metropolitan areas of the country. How do the particular histories and circumstances of these metropolitan areas make the outcomes of the employment systems found within them relatively unique? To what extent do commonalties and differences among them make their employment systems and relationships operate in similar ways or in different ways? To those questions, the next chapters now turn.

NOTES

1. Kenneth Arrow, "The Theory of Discrimination," in Orley Ashenfelter and Albert Rees, eds., *Discrimination in Labor Markets*, (Princeton: Princeton University Press, 1973), p. 10.

2. Eli Ginzberg, *Career Guidance* (New York: McGraw-Hill, 1971), pp. 236–37.

3. *Ibid.*, p. 244.

4. For a more complete discussion of employment systems in the apparel manufacturing, food service–health service, construction, and local transit industries in New York City, see

Charles Brecher, *Upgrading Blue Collar and Service Workers*, Policy Studies in Employment and Welfare, no. 12 (Baltimore: The Johns Hopkins University Press, 1972).

5. For one discussion of this process, see Boris Yavitz and Thomas M. Stanback, Jr., *Electronic Data Processing in New York City: Lessons for Metropolitan Economics* (New York: Columbia University Press, 1967).

6. Marcia Freedman, *The Process of Work Establishment* (New York: Columbia University Press, 1969).

7. See Marcia Freedman, *Labor Markets: Segments and Shelters* (Montclair, N.J.: Allanheld, Osmun & Co., 1976), esp. ch. 7.

Profiles of Five Metropolitan Employment Complexes

The purpose of this chapter is to provide an analysis of the basic structural characteristics of employment systems and the employed labor force of the five major metropolitan areas centered on New York City, Chicago, Los Angeles, Houston, and Atlanta. It focuses on the similarities and differences among these areas in the distribution of employment in terms of industries, occupations, enterprise forms, enterprise size, geographical patterns and transportation systems, age groups, sex, minority groups, and educational attainment. This chapter thus begins to delineate the ways in which the labor markets and employment systems of the five areas are similar and, also, the ways in which they are distinctive.

INDUSTRIAL COMPARISONS

In general, one can best start the analysis of a metropolitan employment complex by reference to the systems of producing units, i.e. to its industrial structure. Table 3.1 indicates the industrial distribution of employment in each of the five areas. Even though there are significant differences among these areas in the proportions which are employed in manufacturing and in some other fields, it is important to note that, purely in terms of industrial distribution, these areas tend to be more similar than different. There were, for instance, relatively small absolute and relative differences among these five metropolitan areas in the proportion of their employment in education, business and repair services, or communications and utilities, though New York tended to lead among the five and Chicago to lag.

One way to roughly indicate the degree of commonalty in the industrial structures in the five areas is to calculate the sum of the minimum percentages for each industry among the five areas. Thus, construction accounted for 4.3 percent of total employment in the New York area, and a higher percentage in each of the other four areas. This 4.3 percent can be taken as the degree to which five areas had a common construction emphasis. Again, the Houston area had 1.2 percent of its employment in printing and publishing, the lowest of the five areas. Thus the degree to which these areas had employment in that industry in common is 1.2 percent.

When such minima for each industry are summed, it indicates that the five areas had 64.3 percent of their employment in common. All the variation among the five areas was within the remaining 35.7 percent of their employment. Thus, variations in the overall nature of their employment systems which might be due to differences in their industrial structures could occur in only about one third of the work forces of the several areas.

The possibility for variation in their employment systems due to differences in industrial structures are less when one compares only two areas at a time. Thus, of the five areas, the Los Angeles and Atlanta areas have the greatest degree of commonalty in their industrial structures, with 86 percent in common and 14 percent of their employment differing. The New York and Houston areas differ the most, with 79 percent in common and 21 percent differing. The Los Angeles area's industrial structure is closest to being an average of all of the five areas; i.e. on balance, it differs least from each of the others. The Atlanta area's industrial structure stands somewhat between New York's and Los Angeles's, while Chicago's structure is most similar to Los Angeles's, on the one hand, and Houston's, on the other.

The similarities and differences need to be examined with greater care. Each of the areas selected for analysis here has a diverse set of specialized activities, and the list of specialties tend to be related to the relative size of the cities. All of them are primarily specialized as centers for trade, finance, business services, transportation, management, entertainment, and professional services; all of them are regional centers, and all serve to varying degrees the national and international economy. The New York area is particularly specialized as a center of national and international finance, insurance, trade, corporate headquarters, communications, advertising, and legal services.

Each of the areas also has a major manufacturing complex. New York has a vast system for the design, manufacturing, and marketing of

Table 3.1 Percent Distribution of Employed Persons by Industry, 5 SMSAs, 1970

Industry	SMSA				
	New York	Chicago	Los Angeles	Houston	Atlanta
Agriculture, forestry, and fisheries	0.4	0.6	1.0	1.3	0.7
Mining	0.1	0.1	0.3	2.9	0.2
Construction	4.3	4.8	4.5	9.4	6.4
Manufacturing	20.7	31.7	27.3	20.5	19.7
Durable Goods	8.3	20.3	19.2	11.0	11.0
Furniture and lumber and wood products	0.5	0.7	1.0	0.5	0.7
Primary metal industries	0.3	2.4	0.9	1.5	0.4
Fabricated metal industries (including not specified metal)	0.9	2.9	3.0	2.4	0.9
Machinery, except electrical	1.1	4.2	2.7	3.0	0.9
Electrical machinery, equipment, and supplies	1.8	5.0	3.0	1.2	1.1
Motor vehicles and other transportation equipment	1.2	1.2	5.4	0.5	5.1
Other durable goods	2.5	4.0	3.2	1.7	1.9
Nondurable Goods	12.4	11.4	8.1	9.5	8.7
Food and kindred products	1.2	2.4	1.3	1.3	1.8
Textile mill and other fabricated textile products	4.6	0.8	1.8	0.3	1.9
Printing, publishing, and allied industries	2.8	3.1	1.6	1.2	1.6
Chemical and allied products	1.0	1.6	0.9	3.1	0.9
Other nondurable goods (incl. not specified mfg. industries)	2.8	3.5	2.5	3.6	2.5
Transportation, communications, and other public utilities	9.4	8.1	6.8	7.8	9.9
Transportation	5.3	5.0	3.5	4.6	6.0
Railroads and railway express service	0.4	1.2	0.4	0.8	0.9
Trucking service and warehousing	1.1	1.8	1.3	1.7	2.2
Other transportation	3.8	1.9	1.8	2.1	3.0
Communications	2.1	1.4	1.8	1.3	2.0
Utilities and sanitary services	1.9	1.6	1.5	1.9	1.9
Wholesale and retail trade	19.9	20.8	20.7	22.4	23.5
Wholesale trade	5.0	4.8	4.8	5.9	6.9
Retail trade	14.9	16.0	15.9	16.5	16.6

Food, bakery, and dairy stores	2.1	2.5	2.3	2.5	2.5
Eating and drinking places	2.4	2.7	3.4	2.8	2.8
General merchandise retailing	4.4	3.2	2.7	3.8	2.6
Motor vehicles retailing and service stations	2.3	2.6	2.1	1.5	1.0
Other retail trade	5.5	5.5	5.4	5.5	5.9
Finance, insurance, and real estate	7.4	5.6	6.3	6.0	9.5
Banking and credit agencies	2.3	1.6	2.1	1.9	2.9
Insurance, real estate, and other finance	5.1	4.0	4.2	4.1	6.6
Business and repair services	4.0	4.4	4.9	3.9	5.0
Business services	2.4	2.5	3.1	2.6	3.4
Repair services	1.6	1.9	1.8	1.4	1.6
Personal services	5.5	5.6	4.2	3.5	4.2
Private households	1.9	1.9	1.1	0.6	1.2
Other personal services	3.6	3.6	3.0	2.9	3.1
Entertainment and recreation services	0.7	0.8	1.9	0.7	1.3
Professional and related services	15.8	15.9	17.3	15.4	19.5
Health services	4.4	4.9	5.6	4.7	6.0
Hospitals	2.4	3.3	3.4	3.3	4.0
Other health services	1.9	1.7	2.3	1.4	2.0
Educational services	6.9	6.6	6.9	6.3	7.3
Elementary and secondary schools and colleges	6.4	6.3	6.5	5.9	6.8
Government	4.6	4.2	4.9	3.8	4.7
Private	1.8	2.1	1.6	2.1	2.0
Other education and kindred services	0.4	0.3	0.4	0.4	0.5
Welfare, religious, and nonprofit membership organizations	1.6	1.2	1.6	1.4	2.0
Legal, engineering, and miscellaneous professional services	2.9	3.1	3.2	3.0	4.3
Public administration	6.1	3.5	4.7	4.4	5.7
Total	100.0	100.0	100.0	100.0	100.0

Source: "General Social and Economic Characteristics," PC(1)C U.S. Census of Population 1970

apparel, as well as a significantly high proportion of employment in printing and publishing. Besides its primarily regional nodal activities, Chicago specializes heavily in the manufacturing of electrical and other machinery, steel, printing and publishing, and food products. Los Angeles is very heavily focused on aerospace manufacturing and the fabrication of metals, and Houston on petrochemicals. Atlanta has significant aerospace manufacturing, but it is also a state capital. Atlanta seems to be focused more than the four other areas on its role as a regional transportation, wholesaling, and retailing center.

Los Angeles presents something of an anomaly, for it does not exhibit the multiple degree of specialization characteristic of very large cities. Nor does it appear to have as large a hinterland to serve as one might expect of a regional center of its size. Its port is surprisingly small to serve a large coastal city. It is, moreover, relatively isolated from other major centers of production in the country. In some ways, the Los Angeles area appears to be very much more a region in and of itself. Water is the crucial resource in the Los Angeles area, and activities and populations that in other regions might be located at some distance tend to be brought together by the need for access to its water system. Moreover, goods and services that might be purchased from some intermediate distance in other regions tend to be produced within the Los Angeles area to overcome unusually high transportation costs. The Los Angeles economy thus seems to be some unusual mixture of a metropolitan area and a larger region. As a result, its national and international specializations occupy less dramatic proportions of its total employment than they might otherwise.

Regional, national, and international concentration on the service aspects of these metropolitan areas is somewhat misleading in terms of the actual weight of their employment. In each of these areas, for instance, manufacturing is the largest single sector and retailing the second, as Table 3.2 indicates. In none of the areas was any other industry responsible for as much as 10 percent of total employment. (Such statements are, of course, dependent on the classification system used. It is conventional to consider manufacturing a single sector, but services, which are a larger employer in the aggregate, are broken into many separate classifications in the Census system. Again, government accounted for over 10 percent in each area, but the Census classifies government employees in a number of industries: health, education, public administration, etc.)

The fact that manufacturing and retailing are, far and away, the two largest sectors in these nodal cities has contrasting implications. The nature of manufacturing sectors tends to differ dramatically among the areas, which may therefore have significantly different employment system effects. Retailing, which tends to serve local populations, comprises roughly the same proportion in all the areas, tends to be similarly structured, and its impact as an employment system may tend to be roughly comparable among the areas.

Among the other smaller industries, there are some comparisons that seem surprising: Los Angeles has a relatively large proportion employed in eating and drinking places and New York relatively few. Entertainment, not a large sector in general, is a relatively large employer in Los Angeles and relatively small in Chicago and Atlanta. The proportion of total employment in hospitals is unusually large in the New York area.

Some patterns among the smaller, relatively ubiquitous industries do not appear surprising. Trucking is important in Atlanta, but relatively limited in the New York area. Private household employment is relatively high in Houston and Atlanta and unusually low in Chicago.

Several other points are worth noting. First, with its rapid growth, the Houston area had nearly 10 percent of its labor force in construction in 1970, nearly half again as large a proportion as in Atlanta, and double the proportion in the other three cities. Second, despite their roles as financial centers, the Houston and Chicago areas have relatively smaller proportions of their employment in banking, finance, insurance, and real estate than do the three other areas. Thirdly, the unusually high proportion of employment in real estate in the New York area reflects a much stronger tendency for people there to live in and rent apartments, and for businesses to rent rather than own the office and other structures they utilize. Fourth, even though it is not a state capital, the New York area has almost as high a proportion of its employment in public administration as does Atlanta. The Houston area, on the contrary, has a relatively small proportion of public administration employment. Fifth, Houston has another distinction; it is the only area of the five to have a significant number employed in the minerals industry and/or gas production. Finally, Atlanta and Houston have a significantly higher proportion of their employment in wholesaling than do the other three areas.

Comparisons of relative proportions of total employment in metropolitan areas which fall into conventional industrial categories fail to deal with other industrial aspects which may be important in employment system terms. First, there is the matter of sheer size. In a large metropolitan area a given industry with a small proportion of total employment may nevertheless be numerically larger than the same industry with a high proportion of the employment in a small metropolitan area. The construction industry accounted for only 4.3 percent of all employment in the New York area in 1970, as compared to 9.4 percent of all employment in the Houston area. However, this came to nearly 200,000 workers in the New York area in contrast to less than 80,000 in the Houston area. Greater size creates opportunities for greater degrees of specialization into subindustries in the New York area. The New York construction industry has a different mix of types of construction, differing size distribution of firms, different technologies, different materials, different seasonal patterns, and different growth trends. These are associated with demands for different types of skilled workers and different patterns of manpower recruitment, development, and mobility.

Secondly, there are qualitative differences among the cities in the precise character of the activities which are subsumed within given industrial categories. Retailing, which accounted for 16.7 percent of employment in Atlanta, or nearly 100,000 persons, has a quite different pattern than in New York, where it accounts for 14.8 percent, or nearly 700,000 persons. Motor vehicle retailing organizations account for only 1.0 percent of the New York area's employment and general merchandising 2.8 percent, compared to 2.3 and 4.4 percent, respectively, in the Atlanta area. Thirdly, similar industries may nevertheless have quite different employment systems in different areas. For instance, unit banking, which is legally required in the Chicago, Houston, and Atlanta areas, means that they have many small banks rather than branch systems as in New York and Los Angeles; unit banking means that promotion ladders are limited and employees may more often change employers in order to advance than in branch banking systems.

INDUSTRIAL CORRELATES: TYPE OF WORKER, ENTERPRISE SIZE, AND OCCUPATION

The industrial composition of an area is directly related to three other characteristics in employment patterns: the distribution as among types of employers, the size distribution of enterprises, and the occupational distribution.

From the point of view of the relative importance of different kinds of employment systems, it is important that nearly 17 percent of all employed persons in the New York area are governmental employees, compared to 15 percent in the Atlanta area, 14 percent in the Los Angeles area, and only 12 and 11 percent in the Chicago and Houston areas, respectively. The New York area has far and away the largest proportion in the local governmental sector, reflecting in part the high importance of hospital, educational, and public administration there. The Atlanta area has a relatively low porportion in local government, but a high proportion of governmental workers overall because of its high percentage who are federal and state employees. Atlanta is a federal regional center, it has other federal activities, and it is a state capital.

Approximately four out of five employed persons in each of the five metropolitan areas is a private wage and salary worker, but Chicago leads (83 percent), followed by Houston (82 percent), Atlanta (79 percent), Los Angeles (78 percent) and New York (77 percent). The difference is even greater if those who are employees of their own corporation or unpaid family workers are excluded. Paid employees of other persons or private enterprises comprise 82 percent of employed persons in the Chicago and Houston areas, but only 75 percent of those in the New York area.

Conversely, 9 percent of employed persons in the Los Angeles, New York, and Houston areas are self-employed or unpaid family workers, compared to 7 percent in the Atlanta and Chicago areas. The high proportion of self-employed and family workers in the New York area reflects the importance of apparel manufacturing; apartment and other real estate operations; physicians, lawyers, and other self-employed professionals; and small business in general. The high proportion in their own or family enterprises in Houston reflects the importance of the construction industry there; in Los Angeles the large number of eating, drinking, and entertainment places contributes to self-employment.

The New York area is also distinctive for having relatively few persons per private establishment: 12.0 in 1973. The average is much larger, about 20 per unit, in Los Angeles, Atlanta, and Houston. The average number of employees per establishment is even higher in the Chicago area, i.e., 23.4.[1]

New York thus presents an unusual pattern with respect to the relative size of different kinds of employment systems. It has the largest concentration of employment in the country, the public sector is relatively larger than in other major areas, and its private sector tends to have relatively smaller enterprises. The first pattern tends to be associated with a high degree of specialization in labor markets, the second is associated with highly organized employment systems, and the third is associated with loosely organized and market oriented types of employment systems.

OCCUPATIONAL COMPARISONS

The linkages between industrial composition and occupational composition are never direct. Variations in the size of a local industry, in the size of firms, in particular technologies, in relative costs, and in the use of inputs from other industries—all may have an impact on particular local occupational structures quite aside from industrial patterns. Nevertheless, the overall implications of the broad industrial patterns previously noted seem to be relatively predictable.

While each of these five areas have a majority of their employment in white-collar occupations, as Table 3.2 shows, New York is the leader at 59.0 percent followed closely by Atlanta at 57.9 percent, while Houston

Table 3.2 Percent Distribution of Employed Persons by Occupation, 5 SMSAs, 1970

Occupation	SMSA				
	New York	Chicago	Los Angeles	Houston	Atlanta
Professional, technical, and kindred workers	16.9	15.0	17.1	16.5	15.7
Engineers	1.2	1.8	2.5	2.4	1.9
Physicians, dentists, and related practitioners	1.1	0.8	0.8	0.7	0.7
Health workers, except practitioners	1.6	1.4	1.6	1.4	1.4
Teachers, elementary and secondary schools	3.3	2.9	2.7	3.1	3.0
Technicians, except health	0.8	1.1	1.4	1.9	1.4
Other professional workers	8.9	7.0	7.9	7.0	7.3
Managers and administrators, except farm	9.1	7.9	9.2	8.8	10.2
Salaried					
Manufacturing	1.6	1.9	1.8	1.1	1.5
Retail trade	1.6	1.5	1.5	1.6	2.0
Other industries	4.9	3.7	4.3	4.5	5.5
Self-employed					
Retail trade	0.4	0.4	0.7	0.7	0.4
Other industries	0.5	0.5	1.0	0.9	0.6
Sales workers	8.0	7.7	7.8	8.4	9.0
Manufacturing and wholesale trade	2.0	2.1	1.8	2.2	2.6
Retail trade	4.1	3.9	4.0	4.3	4.1
Other industries	1.9	1.7	2.0	1.9	2.3
Clerical and kindred workers	25.0	22.3	21.2	18.8	23.0
Bookkeepers	2.6	2.1	2.2	2.1	2.1
Secretaries, stenographers, and typists	7.1	6.2	6.0	5.5	6.4
Other clerical workers	15.2	14.0	12.9	11.2	14.5
Craftsmen, foremen and kindred workers	11.0	13.9	12.8	15.2	12.8
Automobile mechanics, including body repairmen	0.9	0.9	1.1	1.2	1.3

Mechanics and repairmen, except auto	1.5	1.8	1.9	2.0	2.3
Machinists	0.3	0.5	0.7	0.7	0.3
Metal craftsmen, except mechanics and machinists	0.4	1.4	0.9	0.6	0.4
Carpenters	0.7	0.8	0.7	1.2	0.8
Construction craftsmen, except carpenters	1.8	2.2	2.0	3.5	2.5
Other craftsmen	5.5	6.3	5.5	6.0	5.3
Operatives, except transport	9.9	13.9	12.9	10.0	9.5
Durable goods manufacturing	2.6	7.8	6.4	3.6	3.4
Nondurable goods manufacturing	4.6	3.4	3.3	2.4	3.0
Nonmanufacturing industries	2.7	2.7	3.2	4.0	3.1
Transport equipment operatives	3.7	3.9	3.2	4.1	3.8
Truck drivers	1.1	1.5	1.3	1.9	1.8
Other transport equipment operatives	2.6	2.3	1.8	2.1	2.0
Laborers, except farm	3.3	4.2	3.9	5.1	4.1
Construction laborers	0.5	0.5	0.5	1.2	0.7
Freight, stock, and material handlers	1.6	2.3	1.7	2.0	1.9
Other laborers, except farm	1.2	1.4	1.7	1.9	1.5
Farmers and farm managers	0.1	0.2	0.1	0.4	0.1
Farm laborers and farm foremen	0.1	0.2	0.2	0.4	0.2
Service workers, except private household	11.8	10.2	10.6	10.5	9.2
Cleaning service workers	2.4	2.4	2.0	2.4	2.0
Food service workers	3.0	3.0	3.4	3.0	2.7
Health service workers	1.4	1.1	1.4	1.3	0.9
Personal service workers	1.7	1.3	1.7	1.6	1.6
Protective service workers	2.1	1.5	1.3	1.0	1.1
Other service workers	1.2	0.9	0.8	1.2	0.9
Private household workers	1.3	0.7	1.1	2.1	2.2
Total	100.0	100.0	100.0	100.0	100.0

Source: General Social and Economic Characteristics PC(1)C, U.S. Census of Population 1970

trails at 52.5 percent. This undoubtedly reflects the importance of New York's office center and governmental structures and Atlanta's role as a state capital, while Houston has, for a variety of reasons, a relatively limited system of offices and governmental operations. The high importance of white-collar employment in the New York and Atlanta areas and its low importance in Houston is mirrored in the highest proportion of clerical workers employed in the former two, and the low proportion in the latter.

But other factors affect the pattern for other white-collar subgroups. The Los Angeles area has an unusually high proportion of professional and technical workers. This is due to the importance there of the aerospace industry with its high proportion of engineers, scientists, and technicians; the relatively high employment in educational and health services with their large proportions of teachers, nurses, technicians, and other professionals; and the unique role of entertainment and professional entertainers in Los Angeles. The Chicago area trails in professional employment; it also trails in educational employment and is low relative to most of the other five areas with respect to employment in the health, welfare, legal, engineering, and professional services and entertainment.

One surprise is that the Atlanta area outranks the New York area in the proportions of the total employed as managers and administrators, but Atlanta serves as regional headquarters for the federal government, as a state capitol, and as a retailing, wholesaling, and regional office center. Atlanta also leads in the importance of salesmen in its work force, not only in retailing, but also for manufacturing, wholesaling, and other types of firms.

The Chicago area's reliance on heavy manufacturing is reflected in its having the highest proportion of blue-collar workers, 35.9 percent; it particularly leads in the employment of metal craftsmen other than mechanics and machinists, operatives in durable goods manufacturing, and freight and stock laborers. Houston ranks almost as high in blue-collar employment, and, in fact, is the leader in the relative importance of craftsmen, transportation operatives, and nonfarm laborers, particularly machinists, truck drivers, carpenters, and other construction craftsmen and laborers. This obviously reflects the leading role of construction, petrochemicals manufacturing, and trucking in the Houston area. New York is the least "blue-collar" of all these areas; it trailed in the proportion of its employment comprised of craftsmen and laborers. Despite the importance of the apparel industry in New York, it just barely outranked Atlanta in the proportion of operatives in its work force.

The New York area was, however, the leader in employment in the service occupations. It was clearly the leader in the proportion employed as policemen, detectives, and guards, and was among the leaders in the employment of service workers in cleaning, food, health, and personal service activities. These in turn reflect New York's large component of hospitals, a large public sector, a large proportion of the population living in apartments, and a large office system—all factors which directly or indirectly lead to the employment of many service workers. The importance of service occupations in the New York area explains, of course, the relatively limited role of blue-collar workers in the New York area.

In broad terms, these five areas do not seem to vary as much among themselves in occupational as they do in industrial terms. Where the overall index of industrial similarity was 64.3 percent, the overall degree of occupational similarity was 81.3 percent. In part, this reflects the need of every sort of enterprise or organization for occupational groups which bear similar general titles: managers and administrators, for one, and clerical workers, for another. The occupational data present an illusion of undue similarity because workers in quite different employment systems are grouped together. Neither the industrial nor the occupational groupings used by the Census represent precise labor market or employment system lines of demarcation.

In occupational terms, the Chicago and Los Angeles areas are the most similar pair among the five with an index of 93.0 percent. Atlanta and Houston are the next most similar (91.4 percent) and Los Angeles and Houston the third most similar pair (91.0 percent). Thus, these four cities can be linked in order: Chicago at one extreme; Los Angeles most similar to it; Atlanta the next most similar to Los Angeles and Chicago; and Houston quite similar to Atlanta but somewhat dissimilar from Chicago and Los Angeles.

The New York area tends to be the most distinctive. Chicago, Los Angeles, and Atlanta all tend to be occupationally more similar to each other than to New York. The greatest dissimilarity is between New York and Houston, occupationally as well as industrially. These differences are still not overwhelming; the degree of occupational similarity between New York and Houston came to 86.3 percent.

GEOGRAPHICAL COMPARISONS

Geographical comparisons are difficult to make because we lack convenient distinctions upon which all can agree. Each metropolitan economy occupies a unique geographical site which influences the distribution of employment and the residential locations of its work force. Each metropolitan area has a set of highways, mass transit, and other transportation facilities which is unique to it. The economic, employment, residential, transportation, and other systems mutually influence, determine, and interact upon each other through time in a complex system of cause and effect.

Each metropolitan area, moreover, has a particular set of political institutions, with varying boundaries and powers. These boundaries may or may not be used for the collection and reporting of data. The terms usually used—central business district, central city, suburbs, county, and even metropolitan area—have different meanings in different contexts.

Regardless of these difficulties, one striking point about areas is the difference in their population density (a better figure would be employment density, but the general patterns would be similar). The New York area contains over 5,000 persons per square mile, compared to about 1,800 per square mile in the Chicago and Los Angeles areas, 800 in the Atlanta area and 300 in the Houston area. The New York area is highly concentrated, especially in Manhattan. The Los Angeles area, though of a similar size and density to Chicago, is in fact much less centralized.

The transportation systems of the several areas vary greatly in general character. All but Los Angeles tend to focus on one central area, by rail and/or road. Geographically, the four other cities tend to suggest a wheel with spokes. The Los Angeles basic transportation system is a highway grid. New York is unique in the extent to which it relies on tunnels and bridges for transportation among its several parts, for most of New York City is on islands. Three of the metropolitan areas are incomplete versions of the traditional circular shape for a city or metropolitan area: New York because of the Atlantic Ocean in its southwest quadrant and the effect of the wide Hudson River; Chicago because of Lake Michigan in its northeast quadrant and to the southeast; and Houston because of Galveston Bay to the southeast. Atlanta is inland and somewhat of a textbook city, shading off in employment and population densities in all directions. The Los Angeles area is near the ocean, but the ocean apparently has had surprisingly little to do with the configuration of the economic and residential system as the subsequent discussion suggests.

EMPLOYMENT CENTERS

No matter how the boundaries of employment systems are defined in the New York area, employment is highly concentrated in Manhattan. Indeed, employment is concentrated in three principal areas on the southern end of Manhattan: financial, governmental, and related activities near the southern tip, the "garment district" and related manufacturing, warehousing, and transportation somewhat to the north; and the "midtown" area, with shopping, corporate headquarters, financial, advertising, communications, hotels, entertainment, and related activities.

In 1970, some 1.7 million persons worked in Manhattan, or 55 percent of all who worked in the city, over 40 percent of those employed in the metropolitan area, and indeed nearly one-third of those employed in the entire New York—New Jersey region, comprising the New York SMSA and the Newark, Jersey City, and Paterson-Clifton-Passaic metropolitan areas in New Jersey. For its work force, Manhattan draws heavily on the other boroughs and Nassau County. The employment interactions extend directly and indirectly from Manhattan to New York City, the New York SMSA, and the neighboring New Jersey SMSAs as well as to the Stamford and Norwalk SMSAs in Connecticut and the New Brunswick and Long Branch—Asbury Park SMSAs in New Jersey. However, the surprising point is that no more than 10 to 15 percent of the employed residents of such areas as Westchester County in New York, Bergen and Hudson Counties in New Jersey, and the Stamford and Norwalk areas in Connecticut work in Manhattan. Those who do commute into Manhattan or New York City from outside the city tend to live in the newer, unincorporated parts of the outlying areas, and are overwhelmingly managers and professionals. Although there are a variety of port, airport, manufacturing, and distribution activities scattered throughout the rest of the city and region, employment in the other boroughs and counties tends to be focused on local activities, and the majority of those who work in those boroughs also live there. Nassau County has a limited aerospace complex, and some corporate headquarters and related activities are in Westchester County. The New Jersey part of the region has its own manufacturing, mainly electrical equipment, petrochemicals, and drugs. The major port activities in the region are in and around Newark, New Jersey.

The Chicago area employment complex tends to be less focused on its downtown than New York, although more so than the three others. The downtown area with its financial, office, shopping, and related activities is relatively compact, adjacent to Lake Michigan. Chicago has major steel and petrochemicals manufacturing enclaves to the south. Adjacent to these are other steel manufacturing enclaves in Indiana, in Hammond, Gary, and East Chicago. These enclaves each tend to be largely isolated in labor market terms from the rest of Chicago, the Chicago SMSA, or the region, with limited commutation in or out. Chicago's other manufacturing and related activities tend to be strewn out to the west of the downtown. There has also been some tendency for employment in hotels and other businesses serving business travelers to augment the employment center developed at O'Hare Airport.

Chicago depends more on its suburbs for its workers than New York

City, and its employment is a smaller part of its region than in New York. It is similar to New York in being surrounded by a set of smaller, older cities in all landward directions; the commuters into the city tend to come from the unincorporated areas of Cook and the surrounding counties. Overall, however, only DuPage and Lake Counties have significant local employment as well as commutation into the city. All of the counties in the region draw the majority of their work force from local residents, and all but DuPage employ the majority of their resident labor force in local activities.

The Los Angeles area is unusual, as noted earlier, because it does not have as definite a geographic and economic center as most other areas, even those which are "younger" and rapidly growing. Its employment shows up in widely scattered areas, mostly at the ends of freeways or near where elements of the freeway grid intersect. There is an emerging downtown concentration of financial, governmental, cultural, shopping, and related activities in the center of the region near where a number of such intersections occur, but it is relatively small for an area of such size. The aerospace manufacturing complex is mainly in Burbank and the San Fernando Valley to the north, separated from the rest of the area by a small mountain range, with little commuting in or out. A third center is the so-called "Commerce City" of warehouses, trucking, etc. located to the east of the downtown in an unincorporated region, like a hole within the doughnut of the incorporated city of Los Angeles. The port area in Long Beach and San Pedro to the south is also relatively small, considering Los Angeles's size and nearness to the ocean. Other small employment concentrations are in widely scattered locations: the mid-Wilshire district, the Los Angeles Airport, Santa Monica, Westwood, and Century City to the west; Hollywood, North Hollywood and Universal City to the northwest; Glendale and Pasadena to the north; Pomona, Riverside, and San Bernardino to the east; Pico Rivera and Whittier to the southeast; and Torrance and Inglewood to the south.

The lack of concentration is shown by the fact that the city of Los Angeles accounts for only one-third of the employment in the entire region, compared to 49 percent for Chicago in relation to its region, and 52 percent for New York City. Also, while there is considerable commuting into the city, and a great deal of cross hauling, the evidence suggests that the majority of employed persons live relatively close to where they work. There is, in fact, a constant intermixture of specialized and ubiquitous employment areas and residential districts. Quick access to work is also helped because the average speed of automobiles during peak hours is one of the highest in the nation.[2]

Houston, both an inland city and a seaport, lies on a plain extending some 15 to 20 miles from its downtown area. The Houston Ship Channel runs from near the downtown to Galveston Bay some 20 miles east and then to the Gulf of Mexico. Other than the Channel and the Bay, the only geographical barriers are marshlands near the Bay, especially north of the Bay and east of the city.

Houston has a well-developed downtown plus outlying shopping centers, industrial parks, and office parks. However, heavy industry, railroads, shipping, and related activities tend to be located along the Channel and the Bay. Other focal points are at the main airport 20 miles to the north, the older airport close to downtown, and at the NASA facilities in the Clear Lake area.

For local transport, Houston depends almost entirely on its road network, with some 13 arterial spokes feeding into the downtown from all directions, a loop around the downtown area and a completed circumferential highway some five miles out. Houston is a sprawling city, and includes many areas that would be considered suburban elsewhere. It is not clear what proportion of its employment is downtown or along the Channel, but about 75 percent of the jobs in the area are in Houston, and over 90 percent are in Harris County, of which Houston is a part. There is a limited amount of interchange of employment between Houston, the three other counties in the area, and the neighboring Galveston SMSA.

Atlanta extends in all directions from its highly developed downtown area. It has 11 major arterial spokes leading into the center with a loop around the downtown area and a circumferential highway further out, much as in Houston. Atlanta also has a new subway into the downtown. Besides the downtown area, employment is centered in office parks, industrial parks, warehouse centers, truck terminals and shopping centers along the highways, in the aerospace and other manufacturing districts to the northwest in Marietta and Smyrna, and at the airport to the south.

Over half the employment in the area is in Atlanta; nearly two-thirds in Fulton county, including most of Atlanta; and over 80 percent in Fulton and Dekalb Counties. Over half of Atlanta's work force lives outside the city, and the three outlying counties send over 20 percent of their work force into Atlanta for jobs. The integration of the surrounding area and countryside into the Atlanta labor market is suggested by the fact that some 7 percent of those who work in Atlanta live in Georgia, but beyond the boundaries of the SMSA.

DEMOGRAPHIC COMPARISONS

How do the populations and labor forces of these five metropolitan areas compare in demographic terms? Included under this heading are sex, age, race, and ethnic groups.

The population tends on average to be somewhat older in the New York area (median age 31.6 years) than in the Los Angeles and Chicago areas (29.2 and 28.4 years, respectively), while the populations of Houston and Atlanta are distinctively younger (25.8 and 26.3 years, respectively). This reflects the striking differences among the areas in the proportions of their populations aged 55 and over—21 percent for New York compared to 18 percent for the Los Angeles and Chicago areas, and 14 percent for the Houston and Atlanta areas. It is duplicated again in the proportion of the population aged 19 and under—34 percent in the New York area, compared to 36 percent in the Los Angeles area, 38 percent in the Chicago area, 39 percent in the Atlanta area, and 40 percent in the Houston area. Although those in these older and younger age groups tend not to be in the labor force, this age pattern is nevertheless reflected in the employed labor force of the five areas; however, Atlanta's labor force clearly tends to be the youngest. In the New York area, 54 percent of those employed were aged 40 or over compared to 50 percent in the Chicago area, 49 percent in the Los Angeles area, 44 percent in the Houston area, and 42 percent in the Atlanta area. Put another way, 47 percent of the Atlanta area labor force was under 35 years of age compared to 45 percent in the Houston area, 41 percent in the Los Angeles area, 40 percent in the Chicago area, and 37 percent in the New York area.

SEX DISTRIBUTION

Females comprise somewhat more than half the population in each of these five areas, but the range is narrow: from 50.9 percent in the Houston area through 51.5 percent in Chicago, 51.6 percent in Los Angeles and 51.9 percent in Atlanta, to 52.6 percent in the New York area. In terms of the employed labor force, however, the differences are somewhat greater and the pattern is somewhat different. Women comprise 36 percent of Houston area employment, increasing to 38 percent in the Chicago area, 39 percent in the Los Angeles and New York areas, and 40 percent in the Atlanta area. The differences are not great, but Houston is clearly somewhat more male oriented than are the other cities.

MINORITY GROUPS

Conventionally, minority group status has been considered primarily a matter of race, secondarily to include the Spanish-speaking, and only at the third level to relate to other groups defined by national origin and/or religion. On these scores, the five areas differ in dramatic fashion. In the Atlanta area blacks comprise over 22 percent of the population, the largest proportion among the five areas. Atlanta contains no other significant minority group, for Hispanics, Orientals, and other nonwhites total little more than 1 percent. All the other areas have sizable proportions of both blacks and Spanish-speaking people in their populations. Los Angeles is distinctive in having nearly twice the proportion of Hispanics as blacks, while blacks are double the number of Spanish-speaking people in both the Houston and New York areas and triple in the Chicago area. The Los Angeles area population contains the highest proportion of Orientals and other nonwhites (over 3 percent) compared to roughly 1 percent in New York, Chicago, and Houston. (In absolute numbers, of course, the relationships are quite different. Persons of Spanish origin or descendency numbered nearly 1.3 million in the New York area, 1.1 million in the Los Angeles area, about 300,000 in the Chicago area, and about 200,000 in the Houston area, but less than 20,000 in the Atlanta area.)

From another point of view—i.e., the relative importance of non-Spanish whites—the areas fell into two patterns. Non-Spanish whites comprised slightly more than three-fourths of populations of the Chicago, Atlanta, and New York areas, but somewhat less than 70 percent of the Houston and Los Angeles area populations.

These areas also differ greatly in the extent to which their populations contain identified ethnic groups—i.e., those who are foreign-born and those with at least one foreign-born parent. These groups comprised nearly 40 percent of the New York area population and over 25 percent of the Chicago area population. Those born in Mexico or of Mexican parentage are a significant part of the populations in the Los Angeles and Houston areas, but have already been counted as of Spanish origin or descent. The non-Hispanic foreign stock of the Los Angeles area population came to about 22 percent or to nearly 20 percent if one excludes those of Canadian origin. These proportions are somewhat smaller than in the Chicago area. The comparable figures are much lower in the Houston and Atlanta areas, less than 6 and 4 percent, respectively. The New York area's large foreign stock is predominately Italian and Jewish in origin, while the leading groups in the Chicago area are German, Polish, Italian, and Jewish in origin. However, the extremely diverse character of the foreign stock in these areas is indicated by the fact that in neither New York nor Chicago do these identified groups account for the majority of the foreign stock, and no single group accounts for as much as 10 percent of Los Angeles's non-Spanish foreign stock.

There are little data to distinguish among the "white" native stock in these cities, although all have a certain proportion whose rural, religious, and other background or characteristics confer minority status to some extent.

EDUCATIONAL ATTAINMENT

Educational attainment represents one further way in which the members of a population and a labor force may be distinguished. We can compare our five areas on the basis of 1970 census reports on the educational attainment of persons aged twenty-five years or older. The majority of the adult population in each area had at least completed high school, although the precise proportion varied from 62 percent in the Los Angeles area to between 52 and 54 percent for the other four areas (see Table 3.3). For whites, the similar proportion ranged from 63 percent for Los Angeles to 54 percent for the New York area. For blacks, the range was from 52 percent in the Los Angeles area to 32 percent in Atlanta. For Puerto Ricans or the Spanish-speaking, those who completed high school ranged from 41 percent in the Los Angeles area to 21 percent in the New York area.

The proportion who had attended four or more years of college varied from 14 percent for the Atlanta and Houston areas; to 13 percent for the Los Angeles area; to 12 percent for the New York and Chicago areas. The proportion of whites aged 25 or more who had completed college ranged from about 16 percent in Atlanta and Houston, to 13 to 14 in Chicago, Los Angeles, and New York. The proportion of mature blacks who had completed college came to 6 percent in Atlanta and Los Angeles, 5 percent in Houston, and 4 percent in New York and Chicago. The proportion of mature Spanish-speaking who had completed college was approximately 6 percent in Chicago and Los Angeles—i.e., approximately equal to or better than blacks, while in New York only 1 percent of the mature Puerto Ricans had completed college, well below the 4 percent for blacks.

These patterns reflect in part the different age distributions of the areas, for the older the age distribution, the lower the educational attainment. Among young people aged 18 to 24, Los Angeles is the leader and Houston the laggard in the proportion who completed high school; New York is the leader and Los Angeles trails in the proportion who completed four or more years of college.

SUMMARY

In summary, although there are many similarities, each of the large metropolitan complexes has certain distinctive qualities. The New York complex is distinctive for its sheer numerical size as well as its high degree of concentration; high employment and population densities in Manhattan and New York City are made possible by a highly focused, high-capacity transportation system which brings in workers from a

Table 3.3 Proportion of Persons Aged 25 or More Who Have Completed Selected Levels of Study: 5 SMSAs, 1970

	SMSA				
	New York	Chicago	Los Angeles	Houston	Atlanta
Completed High School or More					
Blacks	40.7	39.5	51.7	32.7	32.2
Puerto Ricans or Spanish-Speaking	20.9	31.4	40.8	32.6	*
Whites	53.7	56.4	63.0	55.6	58.6
Total	51.8	53.9	62.0	51.7	53.4
Completed College or More					
Blacks	4.3	4.2	6.1	5.4	6.1
Puerto Ricans or Spanish-Speaking	1.1	5.8	5.5	7.2	*
Whites	14.0	13.1	13.5	15.6	16.5
Total	12.4	11.7	12.7	13.9	14.3

*Too small a group to be relevant.

large area. The New York area's employment structure contains unusually high proportions in apparel manufacturing; in public employment, especially local government; in international and national business, finance, communications, and related services; in white-collar occupations; in self-employment and small enterprises; and in service work, especially in hospitals. The New York area labor force tends to be relatively older than in other areas, and contains a high proportion of foreign stock, especially Italian and Jewish Americans. New York contains both the largest black and the largest Hispanic work force of any city in the United States, but non-Hispanic whites comprise a significantly larger proportion of the total than in the other large metropolitan employment systems considered here.

The Chicago metropolitan employment complex is distinctive in its high proportion of blue-collar occupations and manufacturing, particularly in electrical and other machinery, steel, printing and publishing, and food products manufacturing. The activities concentrated in its downtown area are not unusual for a large city. A distinctive secondary heavy manufacturing enclave in the southeast contains an essentially local labor force separate from the rest of the area. Private sector employment is an unusually high proportion of the total. The Chicago area contains a high proportion of foreign-born (but not as high as New York), mainly of German, Polish, Italian, and Jewish origin. Its black population is relatively large, but its Hispanic population, though significant, is relatively small.

The Los Angeles metropolitan employment complex is distinctive by virtue of the unusually high proportion of employment in the aerospace industry and metal fabrication; in professional and technical occupations, particularly in the aerospace, education, and health sectors; in entertainment and eating and drinking places; and in self-employment. The Los Angeles metropolitan employment system is geographically diffuse. Its downtown is relatively small and many other relatively small employment centers intermix with residential areas, with transportation heavily dependent on a widespread highway grid system. There is also a relatively isolated aerospace complex in the San Fernando Valley to the north. Mexican-Americans comprise the principal minority group in the Los Angeles area, with blacks the secondary group.

The Houston metropolitan employment complex is much smaller in numbers than the three already discussed, but not in area. It has a very high proportion employed in petrochemicals and, because of its rapid growth, in construction. Rapid growth has also attracted a relatively young labor force. Employment is heavily blue-collar in character, and thus male in orientation. Houston has a relatively large black population as well as a significant Mexican-American population.

The Atlanta metropolitan employment complex is based primarily on regional offices, trade and trucking, aerospace manufacturing, and state and federal government. An unusually high proportion are employed in sales and as managers and administrators. Its labor force contains a relatively high proportion of young workers, women, and blacks, but very few Spanish or other racial or ethnic groups. Atlanta is distinctive in having a significant black middle class.

NOTES

1. U.S. Department of Commerce, *County Business Patterns, 1973.*

2. Peter Marcuse, "Mass Transit for the Few," *Society,* vol. 13, no. 6, September/October 1976, p. 44.

Differential Institutions in Five Metropolitan Areas: Their Implications for Labor Markets and Employment Systems

This chapter is devoted to an explication of the apparent effects of a variety of institutional differences among the five metropolitan areas on the way in which their labor markets and employment systems operate. The differentials to be discussed include: the institutional structure as evidenced by the industrial and occupational composition of employment; the nature of employment systems in the private, public, and nonprofit sectors; the impact of size, spatial layout, and transport on the operation of labor markets; and the impact of various other institutional and attitudinal differences, including ethnic and racial attitudes and relationships, union and management policies and practices, alternatives to employment, and attitudes toward work. None of these variables is subject to statistical treatment; Chapter 5 will be devoted to a statistical analysis of the interactions of the differential structures, institutions, and growth rates of the metropolitan complexes on employment patterns in the five areas.

IMPLICATIONS OF DIFFERENTIAL INDUSTRIAL AND OCCUPATIONAL STRUCTURES FOR INSTITUTIONAL PATTERNS

The differential mix of industrial and occupational structures among the five metropolitan employment complexes suggests several direct correlates in terms of the nature of their employment systems and manpower markets. First, we will discuss the implications of distinctive patterns in the private sector. Later, we will discuss the implications for employment systems of differences in the governmental and nonprofit sectors of the several metropolitan areas.

Due to the New York area's specialization as a center for national, international, and regional finance, insurance, trade, corporate headquarters, communications, advertising, and legal services, many New York employment systems tend to be characterized, first of all, by an unusual emphasis on high level talent. Important, though not necessarily large, groups of specialists are recruited nationally and internationally. Some of the most prestigious, large organizations have relatively formal recruitment, selection, and advancement procedures via a highly bureaucratized set of functions, not only for high level, but also for clerical and office employees. This tends to be the case in commercial and investment banking, legal services, corporate headquarters, accounting firms, etc. National and some international organizations have special problems in recruiting and rotating executives, professionals, and specialists into middle level positions in New York and its suburbs because of difficulties with the availability of housing, transportation, and amenities, and the high cost of living compared to other cities and their suburbs. Faced with extensive and expensive commuting times to what they consider suitable locations in Connecticut, Long Island, or New Jersey, as well as the high cost of living in the metropolitan area, it has become increasingly difficult to recruit the talent and potential needed for these systems.[1] Obviously, this varies among fields, types of talent, individuals, and firms.

The major agglomeration of talent is by no means dominated by large, bureaucratic employment systems. Many advanced services are provided by relatively small organizations which shift and recombine for a variety of business and personal reasons. There is a considerable amount of job-hopping and self-aggrandizement of talent at many levels in such fields as advertising, communications, finance, entertainment, business services, real estate, etc.

New York's white-collar employment systems formerly attracted great numbers of young women from across the region and nation, but have been facing increasing difficulties in attracting out-of-town women. New York also long relied on white young women graduates of public and parochial schools and colleges for these clerical, secretarial, administrative, and related positions. In recent years, as the white-middle-class population shifted to the suburbs, as more and more white and black women and men have gone to college and entered technical and professional occupations, employers of clerical workers have shifted increasingly to middle-aged white women and younger blacks and, to a lesser extent, Spanish-speaking women and men.

As with higher level and managerial personnel, white-collar employment tends to fall into two types of employment systems: (1) large highly bureaucratized systems with relatively formal recruitment, selection, placement, training, and advancement systems, as in the banks, insurance companies, and the offices of merchandising, headquarters, and other units; and (2) an immense agglomeration of quite small relatively unstructured offices in small operations of all sorts: manufacturing, independent professional firms, travel agencies, hotels, etc. in which personnel functions are relatively unorganized, advancement is by job-hopping, and skills are acquired essentially via individual initiative.

New York, as Chapter 2 noted, has a huge agglomeration of light manufacturing, particularly apparel manufacturing. The garment industry has a special impact on the New York labor market in a number of ways. The industry is especially affected by two disparate economic tendencies. On the one hand, it is characterized by relatively small enterprises. On the other hand, those small enterprises are exceptionally dependent on the economies of agglomeration. To exist at all in the New York area, these small firms must be close to each other and to a complicated set of other small firms which sell them cloth, notions, and the like; rent them machinery; provide sales and marketing services and wholesaling outlets; rent them space for their showrooms, sales operations, design operations, manufacturing, and storage; provide cleaning, security services, photographic, and other services; and provide services for visiting out-of-town customers in hotels, restaurants, entertainment, and travel agencies.

Although some small manufacturing operations are scattered in Harlem, the Bronx, Chinatown, and other outlying locations, the garment complex is thus focused into a midtown district close to passenger transportation, tunnels for trucks to bring in cloth and other materials and to take out finished goods, financial and other services for the entire complex and its customers. In this center, indeed, competitive and complementary firms tend to cluster into particular buildings and blocks, each of which may be devoted to a single kind of production of men's wear, women's wear, house furnishings, decorating, millinery, etc. There are secondary clusters which utilize common support and supply firms; typical secondary clusters include toys, home furnishing hardware, jewelry, etc.

This cluster thus functions as a large, complex, interrelated labor market and employment system. It relies directly on the intersection of the subway lines, suburban railroads, bus terminals, highways, bridges, and tunnels to bring in and take out on a daily basis the large number of diverse kinds of people in the district. There is a constant churning about of firms, entrepreneurs, and labor supply as individual firms temporarily succeed or fail at whatever it is that they do. Different shops are forming, hiring, laying off, or dissolving, because of individual fate or because of seasonal or longer-term patterns of particular sectors of the complex. The high costs and difficulty of doing business in a central congested area means that there is a constant search for less costly, easier ways to carry on each step on each operation, perhaps by relocation to New Jersey or other parts of the country. Firms that do not relocate often face fierce competitive pressure from the rest of the country or abroad. Thus there is constant pressure to limit pay scales, training and promotion opportunities, and commitments to individuals, except as these are negotiated and contracted for individually and collectively.

The garment industry requires a diverse range of skills, many of which are relatively common and easily acquired. With relatively low wages, the industry has relied heavily on those with various handicaps and facing various degrees of discrimination. The older skilled workers are likely to be Jewish or Italian immigrants; the younger semiskilled and unskilled workers are likely to be black or Spanish-speaking women and men, plus a growing number of Chinese immigrant women.

Chicago's specialization in the manufacturing of electrical and other machinery, steel, and printing and publishing also tends to give its employment complex a special flavor. These industries tend to emphasize fairly modern technologies, employ great numbers of relatively skilled men, are highly organized by unions of skilled and unskilled workers, and have rather high pay levels. The steel industry, particularly, has problems with pollution. Apprenticeship programs for the training of skilled workers are emphasized in printing and some of the steel and machinery trades. The steel industry, particularly, and durable goods manufacturing in general tend to have well-defined seniority, training, and promotion systems. As high wage industries, they tend to be attractive to men with limited opportunities. In the past, they relied heavily on various immigrant groups and in-migrants from rural areas in the Midwest and upper South. While in-migrants long tended to be white, blacks found some opportunities during World Wars I and II, and blacks and to some extent Mexican-Americans and Puerto Ricans have gained better and better opportunities over the years. In part, due to the housing and travel patterns of earlier years, and in part because they accepted the pollution, workers in these industries have tended to live near their work. Thus a pattern of industrial and/or living enclaves exists in parts of Chicago, particularly on the South Side, near Calumet Lake, etc. Workers have been clustered not only by industry, but also by ethnic and racial groups. Recruitment inside these enclaves tends to be by word of mouth via family, neighborhood, ethnic, and racial linkages, while commuting in or out of these enclaves tends to be less common than in other parts of the city.

Los Angeles's special emphasis on aerospace manufacturing, including research and development, lends it's labor markets and employment systems a measure of distinction. While parts of this complex are found in many locations in the area, it is mainly concentrated in Burbank and the San Fernando Valley, separated to some extent from the rest of the Los Angeles area by the Santa Monica Mountains, with passage primarily by a limited number of freeways. To some extent the Valley seems to be an industrial, employment, and residential enclave, characterized by high wages and salaries and limited commuting in or out.

The complex contains one large company, Lockheed, and a host of smaller operations. Lockheed and other relatively large companies are highly complex employment systems, employing diverse engineering, skilled, mechanic, and other categories of personnel. Typically, they employ a wide range of personnel at a particular function—that is, with many grades of engineers, aerospace mechanics, model builders, designers, etc. These define complex placement as well as promotion systems. Employees are recruited at all levels, tested, placed, and advanced according to highly developed personnel systems. Although engineers, mechanics, and others are hired on the basis of skills developed previously in colleges, junior colleges, private schools, and the armed forces, the industry is also characterized by a great deal of apprenticeship and other in-house training at every level.

Employment in aerospace manufacturing and research and development tends to be irregular. The level and character of activity fluctuate irregularly, depending on shifts in war, defense, and international relations, the decisions of the armed forces, and congressional appropriations. Companies gaining contracts may expand as other companies completing contracts reduce their activities and employment. Higher level personnel move to companies to prepare for new contracts; intermediate and lower level people may follow them, particularly when contracts are let. It is common to gain information about possible openings via former associates and superiors, and even to be hired by them. Information and manpower flows are primarily within the San Fernando and Los Angeles complex, but often extend into and from other complexes on the West Coast and elsewhere. The somewhat closed nature of the information and opportunity system in the aerospace complex in recent years may also reflect its failure to grow, and there is usually an excess supply of former workers who would like to be reemployed in it.

Those who are released and not reemployed ordinarily spend considerable time on unemployment compensation. However, since so many employed in this complex are highly able and flexible, they often appear early or later in other less attractive, even more casual employment systems. They constitute a kind of floating labor supply that moves into diverse mercantile, service, and self-employment systems if better alternatives are not available, but who also tend to shift back into aerospace if new contracts come through. Thus the irregularity of the aerospace employment system has an inverse impact on a number of loosely related employment systems, creating shortages in the latter when aerospace expands and surpluses of highly able, relatively casual workers in neighboring fields when aerospace contracts decline.

Houston's focus on petrochemicals gives it some degree of specialness with regard to employment systems. Petroleum refining and chemical plants are very capital-intensive and use a high proportion of engineers, chemists, and skilled workers. Moreover, workers in and around the plants tend to be organized into crews in which the members interact intensively with each other in carrying out their highly technical activities. The crews contain workers at many different levels of skill, which define promotion systems. Workers hired at the bottom are expected to traverse a system of job ladders and eventually emerge at the top. Thus, considerable care is taken in the selection of unskilled workers with heavy reliance on tests and placement procedures. The jobs tend to be very well paid, and employees tend to want to bring in their relatives and friends. Training is primarily on the job, often provided by senior workers in an informal, apprenticelike, ad hoc basis as individuals temporarily fill in for absent members or as promotion becomes possible because of departure or promotion of senior workers or the opening of a new production unit.

The Houston employment complex is also significantly affected by the fact that an unusually large percentage of its employment is in construction. This industry is characterized by a constant flux in the nature and requirements of projects and contracts under way. The irregularity of construction employment patterns is mitigated to some extent in Houston because work is not often interrupted by a hostile climate and because the building boom in the city has been so long-standing. Nevertheless, irregular employment in construction, in Houston as elsewhere, means that workers often seek new jobs through their contacts with former employers, co-workers, friends, and, if they are union members, their unions.

Atlanta's industrial structure is the least distinctive of the five considered here, but it does have some special implications for its employment systems. It has a major Lockheed plant and a high proportion employed in the aerospace industry, but is relatively smaller and less oriented to research and development than in Los Angeles. Although a production center, the Atlanta aerospace sector nevertheless employs a high proportion of engineers and skilled workers; it is characterized by well-defined systems for recruitment, hiring, placement, training, and promotion, defined in part via collective bargaining in the case of production workers. Aerospace employment in Atlanta is characteristically irregular, but without as complex a set of alternatives as other aerospace firms and centers or, as in California, unemployment compensation. Aerospace workers in the Atlanta area do not seem to slip back and forth between the aerospace and other local activities as easily as in Los Angeles.

As a regional center, Atlanta has a significant amount of in- and out-movement by managers, sales, and staff personnel from national, regional, and international concerns. It also has a relatively high proportion of its employment in trucking, other forms of transportation, wholesaling, and retailing. Some aspects of these kinds of businesses have highly formal employment systems, such as in aircraft maintenance for the airlines. The more usual pattern is a relatively open melange of employment systems depending on a mix of personal and informal techniques for the acquisition and development of personnel.

IMPACT OF DIFFERENTIALS IN PUBLIC AND NONPROFIT SECTORS

New York's high proportion of governmental, hospital, and educational employment also means that a high proportion of its work force is in employment systems of a particular sort. Many parts of this system, as in teaching and nursing, are characterized by heavy emphasis on credentials, with limited opportunities for informal advancement into the fields. In health, education, and similar fields, large numbers of professional workers are characteristically employed at essentially the same grade levels. As a result there are few opportunities for promotion, and pay differentials are mainly on the basis of years in service. Except in the higher managerial and professional jobs, pay levels and particularly fringe benefits tend to be higher than in comparable private employment. Recruitment and promotion, to the extent they occur, are in highly formal systems involving tests and examinations, appointment lists, etc. There is a highly organized system of private schools for the preparation for civil service examinations. Moreover, attempts to change any of the procedures and norms in the public examination, selection, and promotion systems are strongly resisted via political action, unions, professional societies, and the courts.

The New York area civil service systems have been very attractive to certain ethnic groups, for a variety of reasons. There is a widespread image of the "Jewish" school teacher, the "Irish" policeman and fireman, the "Italian" sanitation worker, and the black and Puerto Rican health worker.

The importance of state government in Atlanta's employment structure, along with a more or less normal complement of city and federal, higher education, and hospital employees means that its labor market is heavily influenced by personnel practices characteristic of public bureaucracies: formal advertisement of openings; testing prodecures;

formal job descriptions; licensing of occupation; formal promotion procedures, etc. However, the degree of formality and the precision of the system is much less extensive in the municipal, state, and nonprofit sectors in Atlanta than it is in the New York area or even the Los Angeles area. As with many state systems, the civil service or merit system is strongest in departments with a strong federal involvement: employment, health, social welfare, etc. Even in these activities the federal aspirations are often informally abrogated, and patronage and connections play a role. In the more traditional departments, such as highways, the judicial system, taxation, natural resources, and agriculture, there are a variety of informal patronage systems in which the influence of local and departmental personalities and relationships are important for hiring and promotion.

Employment of blacks in the governmental and nonprofit sectors in the Atlanta area has developed in a distinctive way. Atlanta has long been a leading center for black church organizations, colleges, universities, and related agencies. The Atlanta political structure has been unusually liberal for a southern city. Even under segregation there was a fairly well-developed system of black public schools, social service agencies, medical services, etc., resulting in a significant degree of black employment in certain professions, administrative posts, white-collar jobs, etc. As the political power of the local black middle class grew, it gained greater recognition not only in the public and nonprofit sector, but to some extent in some of the leading businesses. This increased even more after blacks were able to elect a black mayor. But the process has never been what might be called fully open. The leaders of the black and white middle classes tend to negotiate changes in the employment structure in both the public and private sector, each being fully conscious of the influence of and implications for different groups in the white middle- and working-class, the black middle-, working-, and under-class, the Georgia state government, and the national scene. In many ways, public, nonprofit, and even private employment systems in the Atlanta area can be said to be as subject to political influence as in Chicago, but with a strikingly different way of operating.

The political and attitudinal structure in the Chicago area has resulted in a surprisingly low proportion of public employment compared to most other cities of comparable size. The power of patronage and the use of political connections for job-finding and advancement in Chicago's somewhat truncated public employment system is evident to a degree not known in other cities. Thus, the role of formal civil service rules and procedures in shaping public employment systems is probably weaker in Chicago than in any of the five cities under analysis here. Formal rules and procedures are kept to a minimum, public notices are rarely made, provisional and nontenured appointments are the norm but can extend for a lifetime, and so on. Surprisingly, pay levels and benefits do not appear to be overly generous, but they seem to be attractive enough to produce a steady stream of suppliant applicants and thankful occupants for the positions the political system chooses to make available.

The strength of the Chicago political system not only envelops the public employment system; it has a significant influence in the private sector as well. The political system controls much that is valuable and often essential to large and small businesses, and commentators often speak of the intimate symbiotic relationship which tends to exist between the political and business sectors in Chicago. Political connections play a significant role in contracts, permits, inspections, traffic control, and other public operations and thus determine which businesses prosper. Political leaders at both the neighborhood and citywide level regularly refer job seekers to a wide range of private enterprises, and this has become a significant factor in who is hired and who advances at every level from the laborer to the executive. Major citywide and national firms cement friendly relations and the receipt of essential services by taking seriously the requests of political authorities. Neighborhood stores, bars, garages, and the like, dependent on avoiding difficulty or finding shortcuts through one bureaucracy or another, find it beneficial to hire ward leaders' friends and clients, including some who are of marginal ability and/or productivity.

Public employment in the Los Angeles area comes closer in practice than any of the others discussed here to the spirit and ideals of merit or civil service systems, with very little conflict and very little exception. Hiring, promotion, and the related practices are highly formal, but convey at the same time an aura of efficiency and equity. The head of the municipal service agency is a respected national figure in the field, a regular contributor to the journals, and co-author of a recognized textbook about civil service systems.

Houston's emphasis on the private sector means that the number of public employees is held to a minimum and that the system has a minimum degree of formality. "Merit" systems exist to the minimum degree necessary in federally associated programs. This is not to say that Houston's municipal employees are unqualified. Rather, power is in the hands of the city's mayor and the executive and administrative officials of the city. They use a variety of methods to acquire employees and promote them as they see fit, given the organizational, personal, and community pressures and resistances which are characteristic of any enterprise, public or private.

IMPACT OF SIZE, SPATIAL PATTERNS, AND TRANSPORT SYSTEMS

The size and the spatial layout of the several metropolitan areas under examination here have implications for the way in which they operate as labor markets. Most new jobs in any employment system are found by direct application, and direct visibility undoubtedly plays a crucial role in job-seeking and job-finding. Knowledge and accessibility are difficult to assess, but direct and circumstantial evidence suggest they differ greatly among metropolitan areas.

New York's huge size means that many aspects of its employment systems have low visibility to the average person. Much New York employment is in multistory buildings, while the principal transportation systems are underground. Thus people can come and go from particular locations with little direct observation to provide information about job opportunities.

On the other hand, New York contains a multitude of fairly specific employment districts, and the location and general character of jobs within each are fairly well known. What is not generally known are the characteristics of particular subcomplexes within, say, the garment, jewelry, or auction business, much less the character of particular employers and jobs within these subcomplexes. Potential employees thus are mainly guided by friends and relatives who work in these places, or else they simply apply at random. Once one gains a job in any area of specialization, word of mouth soon provides information about the nature of employment alternatives within the trade. Indeed, certain coffee shops in the garment district seem to function as sources of job information for particular groups of workers.

There are, in addition, a very large number of employment agencies which, for the inexperienced or experienced, provide essential access to great numbers of employment opportunities. The "yellow" pages in New York phone books have 25 pages of listings for private employment agencies and contractors, almost all of them specialized to some degree in professional, managerial, clerical, and service employment. The degree of specialization is often unusual; some are focused on such fields as data processing, public relations and fund raising, photography, MBAs, export-import, fashion, health professionals and administrators, etc.

Want ads in the daily and Sunday newspapers, and particularly in the *New York Times,* provide a highly effective and necessary market for a wide range of general and specialized jobs. The *Times* has both a very large general run of want ads and special sections of panel ads for professional and administrative posts in universities, colleges, and schools; in libraries; in hospitals and health institutions; as well as for executives, professional, and staff personnel in private enterprises. These ads come from institutions and enterprises in New York City and the region, as well as from throughout the nation and the world. They contribute therefore to New York's role not only as a local, but also as a regional, national, and international labor market.

The problem of locating employers is highly simplified in Manhattan by the very regular layout of the streets north of Houston or 12th Street, but complicated by the irregular street layouts in the Wall Street and related areas, as well as in large parts of the other boroughs. The huge agglomerations in Manhattan utterly depend on the complex system of high-speed subways, buses, trains, tunnels, etc., which bring the working population in from all parts of the city and suburban areas extending into New Jersey and Connecticut.

In New York, work and residence do not tend to be closely associated, although there are many close links. Wall Street, for instance, relies heavily on workers who come by subway and/or train from Brooklyn, Long Island, and adjacent areas in New Jersey. The midtown area relies more heavily on subways and/or trains from Queens, Westchester, and Connecticut. Those who work in the garment industry tend to live along and travel to work via the subways from the Bronx and Brooklyn into and down the center and East Side of Manhattan.

With its huge minority and ethnic population, New York is characterized by a great number of "neighborhoods." However, each minority or ethnic group tends to have multiple centers of residence; neighborhoods are characteristically intermixed, and most neighborhoods contain families which are not from the group which occupies the majority of the housing in the neighborhood. In other words, there are few employment locations in the city and suburbs that are truly isolated from any significant minority or ethnic group.

In the suburbs of New York City, public transport is generally lacking, except for commutation into the city. Thus, those who live in and want to work in the suburbs are almost entirely dependent on automobiles to commute to nearby shopping centers, industrial facilities and parks, scattered office parks and facilities, and the downtowns of older municipalities. In general, however, there is little reason to believe that the New York suburbs differ from suburban Chicago or large parts of the Los Angeles, Houston, and Atlanta areas.

The Chicago transportation system also tends to focus on the downtown area which, however, is proportionately much less important than the "downtowns" of New York. The location and nature of different employers and employment districts seem more open to everyday observation. There, tall buildings are relatively less numerous, and, with one exception, they tend to be smaller than in New York. Transport is more often by auto and bus, and even the rapid transit system is primarily on the surface or elevated, going underground only in the downtown area.

Chicago does not tend to have as sharply defined a set of specialized districts in or near its downtown area although, as noted in Chapter 3, there are a sharply defined set of manufacturing, wholesaling, transport, and other centers in the southern and western parts of the city and metropolitan area.

In large parts of Chicago, work and residence are closely linked, but in other parts they are not. Ethnic communities have traditionally been clustered around manufacturing and related centers in the south and west, and commutation in or out is difficult. Commutation into the center of the city has been relatively good, particularly from the north, but also from the west and southwest. The huge black ghetto to the south, however, has relatively limited employment opportunities in it. Transportation to the center and some parts of the West Side are good. But it is difficult to go from the South Side to many of the industrial enclaves further south, or to the north, northwest, or suburban areas.

Since Chicago is somewhat smaller and more open to casual observation, the job information system would seem to be more open. However, the ethnic enclaves, the high degree of residential segregation, and the relatively high degree of intergroup tension all tend to encourage the flow of information about jobs *within* ethnic and racial groups and to inhibit the flow of information across ethnic and racial lines. This is perhaps reinforced by the nature of the political patronage system which is organized along neighborhood and thus ethnic and racial lines. The number of private employment agencies in the Chicago area are about 60 percent of those in the New York area, or roughly in proportion to total employment in each. Chicago employment contractors serve not only office temporaries, but also emphasize supplying temporary low-skilled workers to factories. Conventional employment agencies focus on not only office workers, but also managers, executives, technical and scientific personnel, and factory workers, in keeping with Chicago's role as a durable goods manufacturing center.

The sprawling nature of the Los Angeles area economy means that most people have a considerable range of choice about where they will work and where they will live. There are, of course, centers and districts where typical kinds of industries and occupations tend to be concentrated: banking and finance in the downtown area, aerospace in the San Fernando Valley, movie and television production in and near Hollywood and Burbank, trucking and warehousing in East Los Angeles, port activities in San Pedro and Long Beach. Nearly all of these activities have secondary and even tertiary centers in the area. Choice of a line of work, therefore, tends to less likely be linked to particular districts in which to work and live than in most other large cities.

Secondly, the Los Angeles area has grown rapidly and in a heterogeneous manner. While there are some older, some luxury, and some fairly run-down areas, near most employment locations there exists a wide range of choices as to the quality of housing and neighborhood amenities. Relatively few who can find jobs reject them because suitable housing is not available, and relatively few are confined to a residential area which is relatively unaccessible to a wide range of employment opportunities.

The only individual with little choice is the person without an automobile. Los Angeles has very little public transportation facilities and no rapid transit. Those without an automobile can be relatively isolated almost anywhere, and there are some concentrations of "autoless" people; Watts has been described as one of these areas. On the other hand, the high degree of automobile ownership (i.e., the proportion of families that have one, two, three, four, or more cars), means that the vast majority of workers and potential workers have a very high degree of personal mobility.

Thirdly, although the vast majority of workers live relatively close to their places of employment, the widespread and extensive freeway system means that those with needed skills and highly specific preferences about both their type of work and type of residence can satisfy both. Some engineers commute from Orange County in the far south to the San Fernando Valley; some bankers and businessmen commute from oceanfront homes to the downtown area; some importers commute from the mountains and the canyons in the north to the port areas in the south; and so on. Commutes of 60 to 80 miles are not uncommon, particularly for those who can avoid the jammed freeways at rush hours or who need to go into their offices only two or three days a week.

Finally, because there is less overt discrimination in housing in the Los Angeles area, various local job markets are relatively accessible. There are significant concentrations of minority populations in the area; blacks in Watts and Santa Monica, and Hispanics in east Los Angeles are a few of the better known concentrations. Those without autos in those districts face particular problems. But mobility into diverse neighborhoods is common for those who get better jobs, especially among Mexican-Americans.

Despite its dependence on surface transportation and the prevalence of the one- and two-story building rather than the high-rise, the location and nature of business establishments is less open to casual observation than might be supposed. Travel is primarily by freeways, which are often located atop earthen "causeways," going through "cuts" in land features, or bordered by trees and shrubbery. Moreover, the freeways often have three or more lanes each way. The result is that much of the time nearby structures are not particularly visible, except for long stretches of uninformative rooftops. Off the parkways and on secondary arterial streets, casual observation is much easier. Even so, many employment centers are surrounded by vast parking lots and others are in culs-de-sac. For an essentially open system, casual information about employment sites and the range of employment opportunities seems unusually hard to come by.

The Los Angeles area has approximately the same number of private employment agencies as does the Chicago area, which means their number bears about the same relation to total employment as in both Chicago and New York. Los Angeles's private employment agencies tend to specialize in clerical workers, temporary low-skilled industrial workers and laborers, and Spanish, Japanese, and other minority workers, generally for domestic service. The importance of internal promotion, reemployment rights, and informal connections in aerospace is emphasized by the fact that aerospace occupations are practically not mentioned by private employment services.

Spatial patterns in Houston and Atlanta are much less significant for the employment complex than in New York, Chicago, and Los Angeles, simply because the former have smaller populations and labor forces. These two smaller metropolitan areas, in population and employment terms, occupy land areas which are similar in magnitude to those of the larger metropolitan areas. Population and employment densities are therefore much lower. Both Houston and Atlanta have relatively well-defined downtown areas. Both have widely scattered employment centers at varying distances from their downtowns, especially in shopping centers, industrial and office parks, trucking and warehouse districts, etc. Houston's major concentration of shipping, petrochemicals and manufacturing, and related industry is along the Houston Ship Channel to the southeast. Atlanta's Lockheed and related manufacturing activities are at Marietta to the northwest.

Both Houston and Atlanta are well served by radial systems of highways feeding into the downtown from many directions and by circumferential highways around the downtown, midway out, and in the outer reaches of the urbanized area. Atlanta has, moreover, a fairly extensive bus system and a new subway system focused on its downtown. Particularly in Atlanta, no residential district is isolated from employment districts to the degree that exists in Chicago or some parts of the New York area; moreover, the interstate highway system is used by a significant number who drive in at high speed from rural areas well outside the metropolitan area.

There is, of course, considerable residential segregation in Houston and Atlanta. Black (and, in Houston, Spanish) neighborhoods are reasonably close to the downtown employment centers, although somewhat apart from the principal industrial areas. Upper, middle and lower income "white" housing districts are found close in, at intermediate distances, and on the outer fringes. Indeed, in Houston, a separate incorporated municipality, Pasadena, whose residents are primarily high income executives and professionals, is located just a few minutes from the downtown area. The intermix of employment locations and lower income residences in Houston is encouraged by a complete lack of zoning, although the residential character of some middle and upper income neighborhoods is maintained by complex systems of restrictive covenants in deeds. In Atlanta, access to a wide range of employment opportunities within a system of residential segregation is possible because of the relatively high development of black institutions, businesses, and private and public service systems inside the black areas, as well as by the transportation system and limited size of the city.

Perhaps because they are rapidly growing, with many in-migrants and large numbers of young and middle-aged workers seeking new jobs, Houston and Atlanta have three to four times as many private employment agencies, relative to total employment, as do New York, Chicago, and Los Angeles. Houston's agencies tend to emphasize engineering, technical, and managerial personnel, and especially their national connections. Atlanta agencies emphasize managerial, sales, clerical, and data processing personnel. Both sets of emphases reflect the nature of their respective employment structures.

INDUSTRIAL RELATIONS, INTERGROUP, AND POLITICAL DIFFERENTIALS

On a whole series of issues which are related to the tone of personnel and industrial relations, intergroup relations, and the political climate, the New York area appears to be the most liberal and the Houston area the most conservative, with Los Angeles, Chicago, and Atlanta tending to fall in the middle in that order. This holds in general for the personnel and industrial relations stance of business managers, for the avidity with which civil rights and equal opportunity are pursued, for the nature of programs for the poor, and for the amicability or rigidity of social and intergroup relations. Chicago is usually considered relatively conservative for a northern city, certainly more so than New York, and generally more so than Los Angeles. Atlanta has generally been considered more liberal than most southern cities and sometimes appears more liberal than Chicago.

New York traditionally has been the center of liberalism, with a long history of support for ethnic, religious, and other kinds of pluralism, equal opportunity, trade unions, enlightened managerial practices, etc. Perhaps a corollary is the relative degree of indifference to the fact that large numbers of illegal immigrants are in its labor market.

The public support of pluralism in New York is, of course, the counterpart of the high degree of ethnic, racial, and religious identification in the city. One cannot but be impressed by the close linkages between certain ethnic groups and certain lines of work. The most recent is the rapid entry of Korean immigrants into small vegetable markets throughout Manhattan. Chinese and Greek cooks now work in many "Italian" restaurants. Put another way, the avowed liberalism of New York as a generalized "credo" is not unrelated to a labor market in which information about and access to jobs is strongly shaped by ethnic factors, often making entry into new fields difficult for minority or new ethnic groups.

New York's labor market is undoubtedly affected by a widespread willingness to ignore the "rules." The large number of illegal immigrants in the labor market means that much of the data about employment in New York is somewhat inaccurate. It also means there is a fairly constant supply of manpower from outside the country, especially for certain kinds of jobs at the bottom of the pay scale.

Chicago ethnic groups have traditionally maintained a sharper degree of ethnic identification with respect to themselves and each other. Chicago is rarely considered liberal, and there has been great resistance to blacks moving into many neighborhoods and suburban areas. However, the fact that so many blacks have migrated to the Chicago area over the decades is offered by some as evidence that it has provided relatively good employment opportunities for them. Whether this is due to relatively more tolerant attitudes towards blacks with respect to employment than housing, or whether it reflects a more blue-collar-oriented industrial structure may be argued. While race and intergroup relations often appear hostile in the Chicago area, on reflection the divisions are less deep-rooted than in Atlanta or Houston.

Los Angeles is relatively free of ethnic identification along European origin lines, in part because its population contains so many in-migrants and long time residents who must go back three, four, or more generations to find antecedents who were immigrants. The main intergroup distinctions involve blacks, Mexican-Americans, and Orientals. Discrimination against these groups, to the extent it exists, seems to be less a problem than does discrimination in Chicago, and in some terms, perhaps, less than in the New York area.

Attitudes toward minority groups seem more sharply defined in the Houston area than in any of the other four under consideration here. Although Houston has some claim to being a cosmopolitan city, it also has attracted great numbers of rural and small town whites who carry over many ideas and patterns learned earlier. In general, blacks tend to be consigned to jobs at the bottom of the scale in terms of pay and general attractiveness. In these occupations, moreover, blacks resist Mexican-Americans who tend to fall into certain lines of work traditional for them in that area: small scale construction, hotel and restaurant service, etc.

Racial attitudes and relations seem most complex in the Atlanta area. The leading business and professional groups have tended to be liberal for a southern city, especially in relationship to the black middle class. There is, however, a substantial white population with relatively hostile attitudes toward blacks. This hostile or negative white population tends to be in lower income, lower status jobs, although such attitudes are by no means confined to those with lower status. The hostile or negative population also includes relatively high proportions of relatively new in-migrants from rural and small town areas in Georgia, northern Florida, Alabama, South Carolina, etc. The complex political interrelationships between the white middle-class moderates, whites who are hostile or negative with regard to blacks, the black middle class and the black working class and under classes has been alluded to above.

The nature of union-management relationships and attitudes varies subtly rather than to a major degree among the New York, Chicago, and Los Angeles areas. The United States Bureau of Labor Statistics reported that as of about 1970, 85 percent of industrial production workers in New York were in plants covered by collective bargaining contracts, compared to 71 percent in Chicago, 70 percent in Los Angeles and Atlanta, and 67 percent in Houston.[2] The New York area is characterized by prounion attitudes, a high degree of union organization, and managerial groups with relatively advanced industrial relations policies. Unions are very important in light manufacturing, printing and publishing, construction, the public and nonprofit sector, and transportation. However, the large number of small firms and high importance of white-collar work means that the role of unions is limited in large parts of the New York employment complex. Moreover, the relatively small firms in manufacturing are in highly competitive industries with limited skill demands. The result is that both unions and management have only a limited range within which to exercise discretion, job control is limited, and training and promotion systems are minimal.

The governmental sector in New York is more highly unionized than in almost any other metropolitan area, and the unions have considerable political influence. The main effect of this on hiring, training, and promotion policies and practices has been to strengthen the high degree to which civil service rules have been developed and enforced. The major exception has been sporadic efforts by unions representing lower status hospital, educational, and social service workers to develop plans for internal upgrading of service workers to technician and entry level professional positions.

The Chicago area, with its high proportion of employment in durable goods industries and intermediate level skilled jobs, is also a strong union town. Because these are very capital intensive industries, there is, in one sense, more room for discretion on the part of both unions and management with respect to manpower policies. As a result, seniority systems, promotion, etc. are significantly influenced by collective bargaining. Since job rights tend to be more clearly defined, managements tend, in actuality, to have limited discretion over who gets promoted. Management in the typical Chicago area industries does, in fact, appear to be relatively conscious of their employees in a human resources sense—i.e., concerned with the careers, skills, and the development of their work forces.

On the other hand, collective bargaining in the Chicago area public sector seems subordinate to the overarching political control of government. Union-management relations in government in Chicago have been characteristically informal. The fact is that the public sector is limited in size, and promotion opportunities are also limited. Promotion and training are unusually subject to systematic but arbitrary decisions by political authorities. It is fairly common for employment, training and promotion possibilities, even when they are based on federal funds, to be held in abeyance until their political and employment implications have been determined in considerable detail.

Union and management styles take on a different configuration in the Los Angeles area. By and large, unions are nearly as important there as in Chicago and New York, and many managements are as progressive. The Los Angeles public sector is more organized than in Chicago, but less than in New York. But there was considerable political and management resistance to unions in even the private sector until little more than a generation ago, and some of those attitudes linger. Thus, considerable segments of the population and many managers are quite conservative. Consequently, there tends to be relatively open, less sharply defined practices with respect to hiring, promotion, training, etc. The two major exceptions are in film production and the networks, which, on balance, differ little from their counterparts in New York, and the aerospace industry, where equal employment practices and significant in-house training have been encouraged by federal contract provisions. Construction and transportation are also highly unionized, with the usual impacts on hiring, training, promotion, placement, etc.

The Houston area is characterized, however, by a much more conservative or less hospitable set of attitudes by employers, employees, public officials, and the general public, and has a much weaker set of unions. Houston might even be considered a nonunion area, with the exception of its petrochemical and other manufacturing, longshoring, and some other scattered activities. The petrochemical industry, moreover, tends to contain independent unions, the public sector is not unionized, and the scope of the building trade unions is unusually limited. Industrial managements tend to retain much more discretion in the Houston area. Even where promotion systems are sharply defined by the technology, promotion rights and criteria are less sharply defined. The results may not be greatly different overall, but the process is often less predictable.

In addition, since Houston and its construction industry have been growing so rapidly, the building trades unions have less control of hiring, training, advancement, job security, etc., than usual. Indeed, the trade unions have concentrated on major business and governmental projects and paid little attention to home building, particularly small homes. Given Houston's almost semitropical climate, small homes tend to be simpler in design and construction. Home building thus tends to be done by small businesses, many of them family concerns, including a high proportion of Mexican-American entrepreneurs with their relatives and friends as employees.

Thus, construction employment in Houston is a curious mixture of barriers, openness, and flux in both major or small projects. There are strong racial and ethnic antipathies on the part of many employers, employees, and unions, and white workers tend to fill the craft and higher level positions and blacks the laboring positions on larger projects.

In keeping with Atlanta's liberal attitudes, unions have played a relatively important role there compared to other southern cities but less than in New York, Chicago, and Los Angeles. Atlanta managements have tended toward a more benign human relations, human resources approach. This is especially true not only in the aerospace activities, but also in the manufacturing, trade, and transportation sectors. Union leaders have often played a role in trying to minimize conflicts between working class whites and blacks, and there has been considerable progress in reducing the degree of segregated unionism once common in its building trades, manufacturing, and other sectors. Tolerant attitudes toward union influence in employment practices and progressive employment practices on the part of management are more characteristic of the leading industries and firms. Outside these strategic, involved firms, much more conservative attitudes prevail.

ATTITUDES TOWARD WORK

Can one compare the several areas with respect to attitudes toward work? The evidence is anecdotal, and needs more careful investigation, but many believe there are significant differences among metropolitan areas.

The New York area is said by some to have a high proportion of employees who are inattentive to work; who tend to take long lunch hours; and who insist on leaving punctually or even early to make their trains. The exodus to the shore or country on Fridays, holiday eves, and during much of the summer are observable facts of life in the New York area. On the other hand, the pace of work and the degree of ambition exhibited by many would be hard to match. Recent immigrants, in particular, seem to exhibit a strong willingness to work.

One rarely hears anything special said about the willingness of Chicagoans to work or the pace of work in the Chicago area. Los

Angeles, however, is often pictured as the epitome of a leisure oriented society. The nearness of the ocean, mountains, deserts, ski country, and wilderness all encourage an active leisure life. Many clearly came to Los Angeles and its climate for a more relaxed way of life, and some are semiretired, though not necessarily old. Others argue that Los Angeles also has its share of extraordinarily ambitious, aggressive persons, both young and old. Still others argue that many workers who lead a strenuous leisure life also work strenuously when they are on the job.

The Houston Chamber of Commerce argues that work attitudes are very positive in Houston, that as a dynamically growing city it attracts people who want to work. There is no doubt that fortunes and rapid advancement can be realized in Houston, and that it has attracted a great many ambitious, hardworking persons. There is also reason to believe that, to the extent a strong work ethic is part of fundamentalist Christian beliefs, these attitudes may be stronger in Houston's white and black population than any of the other cities discussed here. Houston is, however, also very much a leisure oriented city, with a relatively young population, strongly inclined toward professional sports, hunting, water and beach activity, etc. In Houston, a clever person can make a good living without working overly hard and still enjoy the city's night life and weekends.

Atlanta projects a more serious mien than any of these five cities. It, too, has attracted large numbers of ambitious young people and even a high proportion of black and white fundamentalists. But Atlanta seems less leisure oriented than any of the other cities. It is attentive to business, but is more focused on church and culture than Houston.

There is also reason to believe that the alternatives to work differ significantly among these five areas, with an impact on the way in which their labor markets operate. New York has long had relatively generous programs for unemployment compensation, disability and retirement benefits, and public assistance programs. New York also seems to have more highly developed systems of illegal income sources from dealing in drugs, gambling, and stolen goods.

Houston is distinctive among the five areas studied here for the degree of political resistance in it and its state government to various forms of social insurance, such as unemployment compensation, welfare programs, etc. This takes the form of lower benefits and more astringent systems for determining eligibility; i.e., there are relatively fewer beneficiaries on unemployment and welfare rolls in Houston than in most other cities.

There is little evidence to indicate the relative availability of alternatives to employment in the three other areas. With respect to the availability of income flows from government, the five areas appear to be ranked as follows: New York, Los Angeles, Chicago, Atlanta, and Houston. With respect to the availability of illegal income flows, the areas appear to be ranked as follows: New York, Chicago and/or Los Angeles, Houston, and Atlanta. Both Los Angeles and Atlanta try to cultivate a relatively liberal style with regard to forms of social protection, but Atlanta simply has not had the resources or the political thrust to provide benefits on a scale to match Chicago, which is relatively conservative for a northern area. On the other hand, there is reason to believe the degree of illegal activity is a function of size, but that Los Angeles and Houston may have a higher degree of illegal activity than other similarly sized cities because of their proximity to the Mexican border and illegal drug and other traffic. If so, Houston may have a significantly higher degree of employment in illegal activities than Atlanta; and Los Angeles may be the equal of Chicago, which has traditionally been considered a center for organized crime. These are all speculations, however.

CONCLUSION

There is no simple way one can summarize this discussion of institutional differences among these five large metropolitan areas and their implications for the way in which labor markets and employment systems operate in general and for specific groups in the labor force. The cross currents, the conflicting tendencies in different sectors within particular metropolitan areas, the complex interactions between different aspects of the institutional structures in each metropolitan area, all mean that no single scale can be used to weigh their net effect.

Suffice it to say that New York's reputation as a liberal city offering great opportunities to all has, as a counterweight, some industrial sectors and some institutional practices that probably limit and control mobility in a significant way. Los Angeles, while avowedly more conservative, may be characterized as a quite liberal, open system, in fact. Chicago, with a more abrasive style, may provide a relatively more supportive employment system than is apparent on the surface, by virtue of its industrial sectors and some aspects of its political system. Atlanta represents an even more distinctive amalgam of white collar, governmental, and industrial sectors, each with their characteristic patterns, modified by a very complex social, political, managerial, and trade union structure. Houston's apparently more conservative managerial, political, and social system may be more than counterbalanced by an exuberant economic system, providing opportunities for advancement for many who are coming in from less responsive employment systems in other cities, towns, and rural areas. The next chapter presents a statistical analysis which seeks to determine how the structural factors set out in Chapter 3 and the institutional factors discussed in this chapter interact to effect the employment patterns of those who are newly entering each of these major metropolitan employment complexes: those who are in their middle years; men and women; and whites, blacks, and Hispanics.

NOTES

1. For further explication of these problems, see Conservation of Human Resources *The Corporate Headquarters Complex in New York City* (New York: Columbia University, 1977).

2. U.S. Bureau of Labor Statistics, *Wages and Related Benefits*, Bulletin 1725-95, September 1973, app. table 4.

Patterns in Employment in Five Metropolitan Areas: The Effect of Structure, Institutions, and Growth

The preceding chapters described the differential characteristics of the five large metropolitan employment complexes. This chapter deals with the question of the impact of these differences on employment and labor market processes and outcomes. As we shall see, the ways in which employment processes work are also affected by the patterns of growth and decline in employment in particular employment complexes.

As noted earlier, so many factors play a role in labor market and employment processes in each metropolitan complex that it is not possible to use statistical correlation techniques to trace their effects. Rather, when the concomitant existence of several events is noted, the assignment of cause and effect can only be based on the judgment of the analyst. Moreover, when so many factors are considered it is not possible to tease out the full range of effects in each metropolitan area. Rather, what follows is a series of tentative analyses, setting out some of the principal ways in which differential structures, institutions, and growth patterns affect employment outcomes in the several large metropolitan employment complexes.

DIFFERENTIAL GROWTH RATES

As Table 5.1 indicates, the five metropolitan areas considered here differ significantly in the rate at which employment grew between 1960 and

1970. This reflects differences in the underlying economic forces in the several economic areas, rather than differences in their labor market structures and institutions. However, differences in metropolitan area employment growth rates have a major effect on labor market structures and on how labor market processes work.

Rapidly growing metropolitan areas like Houston and Atlanta tend to grow in all or nearly all industrial and occupational categories. Slowly growing areas like New York tend to experience employment expansion in some industries and occupations, and declines in others. In the New York area, the expansion of service industries, government, and white-collar occupations tended to be offset by declines in employment in manufacturing, the private sector, and blue-collar workers. In moderately growing areas like Chicago and Los Angeles, the expansion of service, government, and white-collar employment was accompanied by relative stability in manufacturing, private, and blue-collar employment.

These industrial, occupational, and public vs. private sector growth patterns were linked in turn to the character of the net additions to the employed labor force in these areas. Houston and Atlanta, where there was a broad expansion in not only construction, manufacturing, utilities, and the like, but also in the services and government, tended to rely very heavily on males and on whites as new entrants in their labor force, as Table 5.2 shows. These patterns were stronger in Houston than in Atlanta, perhaps because Houston is more "blue-collar" in character than Atlanta.

In the New York area, both because of its white-collar character, and because its white-collar sector was growing while its manufacturing and blue-collar sectors were declining, the net additions to its employed work force were either females or minority males. Employment of white males declined between 1960 and 1970. Moreover, significant numbers of males who were aged twenty-five and above and employed in New York in 1960 were no longer employed there in 1970, as Table 5.3 shows. Some had undoubtedly moved to other areas. The evidence also suggests that

---

Table 5.1 Total Employment, and Percent Change, 5 SMSAs, 1960 to 1970

Area	1960	1970	Change Number	Change Percent
New York	4,372,640	4,631,311	258,671	5.9
Chicago	2,511,564	4,280,251	368,687	14.7
Los Angeles	2,373,691	2,845,532	471,841	19.9
Houston	526,188	804,338	278,150	71.0
Atlanta	395,190	592,412	197,222	49.9

Table 5.2 Net Change in Employment by Sex and Race, 5 SMSAs, 1960 to 1970

Area	Total Change	Males			Females		
		Total	White	Nonwhite	Total	White	Nonwhite
New York	258,671	−18,173	−85,150	66,977	276,844	201,483	75,361
Chicago	368,687	112,322	71,289	41,033	256,365	195,053	61,312
Los Angeles	471,841	182,644	174,763	7,881	289,197	258,138	31,059
Houston	278,150	156,312	136,342	19,970	121,838	100,069	21,769
Atlanta	197,222	104,636	88,347	16,289	92,586	72,396	20,190

retirements and withdrawals from the labor force tend to occur earlier in New York than elsewhere. (Indeed, there is other evidence that some males who were too young to be in the labor force in 1960 were already located elsewhere by 1970, either after brief employment in New York in the interim or after finishing high school, college, or graduate school in some other part of the country.) This not only reflects the slow growth of employment in the New York area, but also the fact that so many workers lost jobs in firms that failed or moved, the greater difficulty in gaining reemployment in the New York area if one becomes unemployed, and the greater availability of pensions, unemployment compensation, welfare, and other income flows when not employed.

The fact that minority groups provided roughly half of the net growth in employment in the New York area between 1960 and 1970 seems to flow from a complicated set of factors. Shrinkage of employment in manufacturing and related activities undoubtedly tended to depress the employment of minorities in the area. However, many minority workers found employment in the expansion of health and hospital services and of auxiliary activities in schools and colleges.

In addition, minority workers made significant gains in clerical and other better jobs because those fields were expanding, because of relatively liberal attitudes in New York profit and nonprofit enterprises, because of the growing political influence of minority groups, and because affirmative action programs were more willingly accepted and supported there than in many other cities. In addition, educational levels of new minority workers were rising rapidly; the former inflow of educated young white men and women turned to a net outflow, particularly of white men; and members of minority groups in the New York area seemed less able or less willing to risk entering the labor market in the South and West.

The age at which young men enter the labor force seems to be related to the growth rate of employment in an area, but also to other factors. As Table 5.4 indicates, young men in New York tend to enter the labor force at a distinctly later age than in any of the other areas. Besides the slow growth of employment in New York, this may also be related to several other facts: the expanding white-collar and governmental areas of employment tend to have higher educational standards for entry; educational standards in all fields tend to be higher in New York than elsewhere; educational institutions there have focused on retaining students in school via elaborate systems of both remedial education and more or less automatic promotion; a widespread system of public community and senior colleges; open enrollment programs in higher education; and unusually high availability of welfare benefits and illegal income.

Some other artifacts of rapid growth vs. slow growth are worth noting.

Table 5.3 Cohort Analysis of Employment Changes by Sex and Age, 5 SMSAs, 1960 to 1970

	New York	Chicago	Los Angeles	Houston[a]	Atlanta
Net Change in Employment	258,671	368,687	471,841	333,886	197,222
Net Change in Male Employment	-18,173	112,322	182,644	197,197	104,636
Cohorts, by 1970 age					
14-23	330,898	255,128	250,643	89,991	59,135
24-29	281,070	171,222	183,183	70,001	49,120
30-34	84,262	55,384	64,720	32,683	18,124
35-44	-3,082	4,915	7,077	31,179	11,977
45-54	-71,359	-33,848	-38,556	13,663	1,428
55-64	-165,763	-88,590	-85,520	-2,070	-10,742
65-74	-346,509	-183,683	-147,706	-22,672	-18,062
75-84	-112,405	-59,858	-44,199	-5,769	-5,418
85 and over	-15,285	-8,348	-6,998	-809	-926
Net Change in Female Employment	276,844	256,265	289,197	136,689	92,586
Cohorts, by 1970 age					
14-23	347,050	245,867	222,874	61,188	53,065
24-29	113,873	67,224	104,847	36,130	30,049
30-34	-35,307	-4,409	15,242	11,519	4,744
35-44	65,967	59,824	59,356	25,962	14,441
45-54	63,486	37,431	23,306	12,871	6,840
55-64	-70,870	-39,492	-35,074	673	-3,606
65-74	-156,135	-81,821	-75,687	-9,034	-10,085
75-84	-46,272	-25,276	-22,873	-2,416	-2,714
85 and over	-4,948	-2,983	-2,794	-204	-148

[a]Harris County only.

Since in-migration tends to occur primarily under age thirty, rapid growth areas like Houston and Atlanta tend to have a much younger population and labor force than the New York area. Since young people tend to stay in school longer than did their elders, a rapidly growing metropolitan area tends to have a more highly educated labor force. In Houston, however, this tendency is somewhat offset by the blue-collar nature of its employment markets and the general pattern of lower educational achievement there as compared to other cities. Chicago's moderate growth rate, its somewhat blue-collar orientation, and its relatively low educational aspirations tend to hold down the average educational level of its workers. New York's slow growth rate results in a population and labor force that are relatively old. The low educational status of this relatively old population is counterbalanced by the fact that so many in this white-collar and professional center are high school and college graduates. On balance, therefore, the educational patterns which should otherwise flow from the differential growth rates of the several areas are offset by educational and occupational factors, and the areas differ little overall in terms of the educational levels of their respective work forces.

Each of these metropolitan employment complexes also differs significantly in the nature of the areas from which they draw in-migrants. Each area draws from its nearby region, but Los Angeles relies heavily on the north central states. New York also attracts Puerto Ricans and both legal and illegal immigrants from all parts of the world, including

Table 5.4 Percent in Labor Force by Sex and Age, 5 SMSAs, 1970

	New York	Chicago	Los Angeles	Houston	Atlanta
Male:					
16 and 17 years	25.3	41.2	34.9	35.9	38.2
18 and 19 years	48.3	65.3	64.1	62.6	60.9
20 and 21 years	62.2	75.2	75.0	77.6	74.2
22 to 24 years	81.0	86.6	85.0	87.0	89.4
25 to 34 years	91.9	94.8	92.8	94.5	95.0
35 to 44 years	93.7	95.6	94.6	95.9	94.7
45 to 64 years	88.7	91.0	88.1	90.4	88.1
65 years and over	29.7	29.2	24.8	30.5	30.6
Female:					
16 and 17 years	21.9	34.4	20.0	18.5	23.7
18 and 19 years	48.3	58.9	52.8	46.7	51.0
20 and 21 years	57.6	62.3	60.6	55.8	62.2
22 to 24 years	57.9	59.9	59.7	56.9	65.4
25 to 34 years	41.6	45.2	50.4	47.6	53.6
35 to 44 years	47.0	50.3	53.3	50.3	55.4
45 to 64 years	50.4	52.3	50.6	46.6	52.5
65 years and over	11.7	12.3	9.9	11.8	12.0

many black immigrants. Los Angeles also attracts immigrants from many countries, including illegal immigrants from Mexico. Houston, Atlanta, and Chicago have relatively limited inflows of immigrants, but do draw heavily on the nearby states in their respective regions.

ENTRY JOBS AND THE IMPACT OF EMPLOYMENT SYSTEMS

The impact of the differential employment systems in large metropolitan complexes increases with age. The several metropolitan areas differ little in terms of the jobs held by those who work prior to high school graduation. As young people complete high school, community college, college, or graduate school, they increasingly tend to enter the distinctive employment systems in each metropolitan area which provide them with access to the better jobs in that area. Entry to the distinctive employment systems of each area not only increases with age and employment, it is also more characteristic of men than women, and of whites than minority groups.

Put another way, employed teenagers under age eighteen tend to be employed in about the same types of jobs in each of the five metropolitan complexes studies here. The differentiation among the cities increases as new entrants come out of each successive level of school. The differentiation between men and women and between the majority and minority groups increases with age in each of the metropolitan employment complexes studied here. The differentiation among the cities increases as

The employment patterns of young men and women under age eighteen were relatively unaffected by the industrial and occupational differences among the five areas. Retail and trade firms were their primary employers in all five, with the proportion in each slightly higher for the young men than for the young women. In all of the areas, moreover, manufacturing firms were the second ranking employers of young men under eighteen, while professional and related service organizations were the second most important employers of young women under eighteen. The young men were employed mainly as laborers, service workers, operatives, and clerical workers, while the young women were employed as clerical, sales, and service workers. While black and Hispanic young men and women under eighteen were employed in somewhat larger proportions than whites in less attractive jobs, the differences were not great.

The major exceptions were the high proportions of young males, especially blacks, in clerical occupations in the New York area. New York has an unusually high proportion of clerical employees in general, but these young men tended to be in messenger and other menial clerical jobs which provide little access to better jobs later in life. Unusually high percentages of employed black young men under eighteen in

Atlanta and employed black young women under eighteen in Houston—roughly half in each case—were in service occupations, again with limited promise for the future.

Even by age nineteen, when most young people have graduated from high school and entered employment, there is little differentiation among the metropolitan complexes in the industrial and occupational patterns for young men and women. The largest single group in each city were those employed in wholesale and retail trade, which tend to have market oriented, loosely structured employment systems. The second ranking field for young men aged eighteen and nineteen in each area was manufacturing, which tends to have more firmly defined employment systems. In Chicago in 1970, indeed, 30 percent of such young men were employed in manufacturing. The second ranking industries for young women were more heterogeneous: finance, insurance, and real estate in New York, manufacturing in Chicago, and professional and related service organizations in Los Angeles, Houston, and Atlanta. Most of these young women were employed as clericals, with smaller groups in service, sales, and other occupations. Most of these occupational and industrial fields provide little training and advancement to their women employees.

By age twenty-five, most men and women who will graduate from high school, community college, or college have done so and entered employment. Such individuals have by and large entered employment systems. Since the employment structures of several cities studied here are more alike than different, employment patterns are more alike than different among the five metropolitan areas.

However, each of the metropolitan areas does have its distinctive industrial and occupational fields with their characteristic employment systems. In each metropolitan area, white males tend to be more heavily employed in the distinctive fields of the area and to gain access to the better and more protected positions in these distinctive employment systems. For example, white males in New York tend to be found more often in the better jobs in finance, insurance and real estate, in government, and in the professional services. In Chicago, white males gain greater access to heavy manufacturing, transportation, and utilities, and their rewarding, upward-mobility-oriented employment systems. In Los Angeles, white men gain the inner track in the aerospace complex. In Houston, they do the same thing in the petrochemical and skilled construction fields. In Atlanta, white males early gain access to the better jobs and employment systems in government administration, private branch offices, and craft occupations.

The employment patterns of women are less distinctive among the metropolitan areas, and, in general, they gain less access to those employment systems which lead to better jobs. Approximately 55 percent were in clerical fields in all areas, with New York a slight leader. Clerical work tends to be relatively stable, but does not offer great upward mobility. The second ranking field for employed women in each city were the professional and technical occupations: teaching, nursing, health technicians, etc. These fields are highly structured, employment is stable, and salaries are reasonable, but upward mobility is limited.

Minority groups in general do less well, of course, than majority groups. The differences between whites, on the one hand, and blacks and Hispanics on the other, are very little among those who are working prior to high school graduation, but increase later. In general this means that minority males gain access less often to the preferred fields and employment systems than white males. It also means that young minority females less often gain access to such semiprotected fields as the "female" professions and to clerical work than do white women. Rather, they are more often found in fields which provide little upward mobility, as in service work in hospitals, restaurants, hotels, institutions, and the like.

Young members of minority groups come closest to entering the same fields as whites in the New York and Los Angeles areas. They tend to lag somewhat behind whites in Chicago. The differences between entering majority and minority groups are somewhat greater in Houston and Atlanta, with one major exception. Mexican-Americans in Houston generally fare better, compared to whites, than do either blacks or Hispanics in New York, Los Angeles, and Chicago. Mexican-Americans in Houston enjoy significant opportunities in small business and construction. Of course, these activities are not part of well-structured employment systems and are relatively open to market forces, but they do enjoy a certain stability based on local custom.

GROWTH, INSTITUTIONS, AND MOBILITY AFTER AGE TWENTY-FIVE

By age twenty-five or thirty, the white men in each large metropolitan employment complex seem to be fairly well-established in the occupational and industrial fields which contain the employment systems which provide stability and mobility and which are distinctive to that area. The possible exceptions are the professional and managerial occupations which require somewhat longer periods of education and experience. Even in those cases, the men were largely in the educational programs, whether in medicine, law, business, or academia, which will provide them with the credentials to enter the mainstream in their respective fields.

A small number of men continue to advance toward better jobs via job-hopping in market oriented fields or moving upward through employment systems.

The degree of mobility after thirty or so is directly related to the rate of expansion of metropolitan employment complexes. As noted earlier, the New York employment complex was growing slowly and during the 1960s gained male workers up to about age thirty-five, but among older men experienced a net loss via out-migration, disability, and retirement. Chicago and Los Angeles complexes gained male workers up to about age forty-five and lost men who were older, primarily through disability and retirement. Rapidly growing Houston and Atlanta gained male workers up to about age fifty-five, after which early and normal retirements led to attrition.

Within these overall growth patterns, each metropolitan complex had its own particular pattern of occupational progressions for men as they grew older. In New York, the number of men employed as laborers, operatives, and clericals increased up to age twenty-nine, as salesmen and craftsmen up to age thirty-four, and as professionals, managers, and service workers up to age forty-four. The pattern was roughly the same in Chicago, except that the number employed as salesmen, craftsmen, operatives, and service workers continued to increase among men five to ten years older. In more rapidly growing Los Angeles, Houston, and Atlanta, the number of men employed as professionals, managers, salesmen, clerical workers, and craftsmen continued to increase up to about age fifty-five. There were a few exceptions. The number of salesmen and craftsmen did grow beyond age forty-four in Los Angeles; the number of male clerical workers continued to increase up to age sixty or so in Houston.

The pattern was more stable for women. Employment of women in all of these areas and in most occupational fields continued to increase up to past age fifty. There were exceptions, related somewhat to the growth rates of the several areas. The number of women employed as operatives failed to increase past age twenty-nine in the New York area, reflecting perhaps the decline of manufacturing in the city. The number of women employed in Houston and Atlanta as professionals, as laborers, and as service workers continued to increase up to about age sixty, reflecting the rapid growth and large minority population in those cities.

The larger significance of these findings needs explication. In a slow growth metropolitan economy like that of the New York area, advancement possibilities tend to be limited. Therefore, one's long-run career and employment status seems much more determined by the employment system which one enters as a young person. This means that both education and whether one can gain access to favorable employment systems are much more crucial in New York than in rapidly growing areas. The ethnic nature of many New York employment systems, the general lack of information about civil service jobs, and the unusually small size of the typical New York enterprise are all part of a pattern in which access tends to be restricted to "insiders," while outsiders often face difficulty in finding a new job.

Many New Yorkers also tend to be locked into their jobs because of the character of the local economy. Although some employment systems are expanding, and some employment systems are being newly established, an unusually high proportion of employment systems are declining, dying, or being relocated to other areas. In these latter situations, there is limited upward mobility. Such stagnant areas include many manufacturing, transportation, wholesaling, retailing, and warehousing firms. In many situations, workers and the enterprise employing them are aging together; there is often a kind of contest as to whether workers will withdraw, leading to the death of the enterprise, or whether the enterprise will withdraw, leaving the workers jobless and facing premature retirement.

In a moderately growing metropolitan employment complex, a greater proportion of employment systems are likely to be growing. This means that upward employment mobility is likely to continue to a later age. In Chicago and Los Angeles, for instance, the number of men who were becoming craftsmen, foremen, and salesmen continued to increase up to about age forty-four in 1970, compared to only about age thirty-four in the New York employment complex. One can postulate that moderately growing organizations and employment systems will tend to promote from within. In cities like Chicago and Los Angeles, one can suspect that entry to and information about employment systems will be closely guarded, with the added motivating factor that if one gains entry to the right systems, one can have expectations of substantial advancement.

The importance of initial entry may be less in rapidly growing areas like Houston and Atlanta. Many employment systems are growing. New firms, organizations, and systems are being established. Job opportunities and information are less guarded. There are unusual opportunities for upward mobility. Some will move upward through organizations, but there will also be great opportunities to move up by judicious selection of opportunities to job-hop from firm to firm and system to system, each time to a better position. The complex contains many young people, and there will be a great deal of churning about as some seek new and better positions, and others leave jobs where they did not succeed. Some of the better jobs will be filled by young and older persons who are shifted into new or expanded offices of national firms and organizations. Many other older in-migrants will find employment opportunities at all occupational levels in such rapidly expanding fields. In general, employment systems in rapidly expanding employment complexes like those in Atlanta and Houston will be more porous. Educational and other criteria for selection are likely to be less rigidly enforced. Information is likely to be relatively scarce, however, because so many employment systems and workers are likely to be relatively new to the area.

INTERACTIONS AND EMPLOYMENT PATTERNS
OF MEN, WOMEN, AND MINORITIES

Growth is, of course, only one of the factors that affect how metropolitan employment complexes operate with respect to different groups in the labor force. Here we turn to more detailed examination of similarities and differences among the employment patterns of men and women and minority groups in the five metropolitan complexes under examination here.

First, the differences in the occupational patterns of men and women were greater than those between racial and language groups in each of the five areas. Sex conventions were the overriding factor in each area, and especially so in New York, Chicago, and Los Angeles, and among Mexican-Americans in Houston. Only in Houston and Atlanta were employment differentials nearly as great for blacks as for women.

Second, the differences between whites and blacks were least in Los Angeles, New York, and Chicago, and significantly greater in Houston and Atlanta. Thus, differential growth rates seem not to overcome what are considered to be traditional racial differences among these areas. The differences between whites and Hispanics were least in Houston, with Los Angeles second, and greatest in New York and Chicago. This contravenes the conventional wisdom that New York is more liberal than southern and western cities with respect to minority groups. Perhaps, the greater use of formal educational requirements (tests, etc.) by both public and private employment in the New York area acts to the particular disadvantage of those with Spanish language backgrounds.

Several unusual patterns deserve mention. Women are usually more likely than men to be employed as operatives, but the reverse holds true in Houston. Relatively few women are employed as managers and administrators in Atlanta where an unusually large proportion of the labor force is in those occupations. Los Angeles tends to have an unusually greater proportion of male than female professionals and technicians, reflecting the high proportion of males in those occupations in the aerospace industry.

In comparing the occupational distributions of white women to black and Hispanic women in the five areas, the higher proportion of whites in clerical jobs was found to be the major difference. There were also consistently higher proportions of white women in professional, sales, and managerial positions. New York had an unusual disparity between the proportions of white and minority women in professional and technical occupations, which are unusually important employment fields there. Houston and Atlanta employed remarkably small proportions of black women as clericals. It would be hard to determine the extent to which these patterns reflect educational differentials, language problems, different attitudes toward minority women in these cities, and different attitudes toward clerical work by minority women in the several cities.

The general tendency for black males to fare relatively better in New York, Los Angeles, and Chicago was reversed in some higher ranking occupations. Black males comprised relatively higher proportions in Atlanta and Houston than in Chicago, Los Angeles, and New York in such occupations as college and school teachers, school and public administrators, physicians, pharmacists, and self-employed managers. This reflects the historically strong position of the black middle class in Atlanta, but also the historical legacy of segregated schools, universities, and public services there and in Houston. In addition, blacks are severely underrepresented in such occupations in New York, and to a lesser extent in Los Angeles, because of the heavy reliance on educational credentials and testing mechanisms in those areas. Chicago tends to employ a relatively unusual proportion of black males as elementary school teachers and public administrators, perhaps because that city and area tends to be unusually segregated for a northern metropolis; because credentials and standards are less stringently enforced there; and perhaps because the patronage system prevails to some extent in the black as well as in the white community. Chicago employs remarkably fewer black males than the other cities in certain fields such as college teaching, architecture, and self-employed construction managers. In 1970, the New York area also had surprisingly few black postal workers, and Chicago had surprisingly many. Again, a complex of factors—attitudinal, political, and economic—must lead to these contradictory results.

In the craft occupations, particularly construction, New York and Chicago tend to have relatively lower representations of black males than does Atlanta. Trade unions and their control of entry into these fields has been stronger in the northern than the southern cities. The situation was often mixed, however. In New York, significant proportions of black males were employed as carpenters and plumbers. In Houston, few black males were employed as painters and paperhangers, but many were employed in the metal trades. In Atlanta, relatively few black males were employed as carpenters. The point is that the impact of restrictions and barriers to entry varies from field to field.

The list of unusual patterns could be extended indefinitely. For instance, relatively few black males are employed as taxi drivers and chauffeurs in New York, but unusually high percentages as cooks, guards, and health service workers. In Chicago, significant numbers of black males are employed as bus drivers, policemen, and detectives, suggesting a certain political influence. Los Angeles has very few black firemen. In Atlanta, a low proportion of black males are employed as bus drivers, policemen, and guards, but a high proportion as firemen, suggesting the differential impact of black political influence in those cities.

As for Hispanic males, though they generally do fairly well in Houston, relatively few were employed as teachers, school administrators, self-employed businessmen in wholesale and retail trade, foremen, telephone and power servicemen and linemen, and tool and die makers. In the New York area, on the other hand, Puerto Rican men generally were severely underrepresented in the higher ranking jobs, but an unusually high proportion were self-employed in wholesale and retail trade, or employed as health technicians and air-conditioning, heating, refrigeration, and automobile mechanics. In general, however, fairly representative numbers of Hispanic men were employed in the various skilled occupations in all four metropolitan areas with significant numbers of Hispanics, with Atlanta being the exception.

Although at a disadvantage in all five cities, black women do fairly well in Chicago, Los Angeles, and New York. However, they are underrepresented to an unusual degree among secondary school teachers, school administrators, and librarians in the New York area, while unusually high proportions are employed there as nurses, dietitians, bank tellers, bookkeeping and billing machine operators, secretaries, and telephone operators. Equal employment opportunity appears to be much more the norm in the private sector than the public sector in the New York area. Unusually low proportions of Puerto Rican women in New York were employed as teachers, librarians, and school administrators. In Atlanta and Houston, black women comprise unusually high proportions of librarians, teachers, and school administrators.

The conclusion is clear. Each major metropolitan employment complex is an admixture of that which is common to all cities, or to all cities of certain industrial or demographic characteristics. Each major metropolitan employment complex also contains institutions and patterns which are distinct or unique to it. The way in which these institutions operate is profoundly influenced by the growth rate of local employment and the way in which its structure is changing, but historical institutional patterns persist. The next chapter presents a conceptual reformulation or summary of how, based on this analysis, major metropolitan employment complexes appear to be similar, and of the ways in which they are often dissimilar.

CHAPTER
6

A Conceptual Reformulation of Large Metropolitan Employment Complexes

This chapter is both a summary and an extension of the analysis of the preceding chapters. The purpose of the chapter is to present a conceptual framework which encompasses both the commonalties and distinctions among large metropolitan employment complexes and is thus applicable to them in general. It is based on the preceding chapters, and those who have followed the argument closely will find its essential findings reproduced here.

First, employment and labor market processes and patterns in a large metropolitan area exhibit much that is common to the other large metropolitan areas, but also tend to be distinctive in part.

The common aspects reflect each city's need of a wide range of common activities to serve both its economic base and its residential population: retailing, utilities, transportation, education, health and social services, municipal services, repair services, local banking, and certain kinds of manufacturing such as automobile assembly, baking, bottling of soft drinks, etc.

There may be variations in the relative importance of even these "common" activities. For instance, the New York area relies far more heavily on public transit than other areas. Thus, it has a relatively small proportion of its work force employed in the "common" activities of automobile assembly, retailing, and repair services. Similarly, Houston consistently employs a small proportion of its labor force in municipal, welfare, and social services, while the New York area tends to employ high proportions in these "common" activities.

The distinctive aspects of a metropolitan employment complex flow in part from differences in its industrial composition and in part from differences in such other parameters as its growth rate, spatial configuration, demographic composition, and a variety of informal and formal institutional elements, including work and life styles, political structure, industrial and ethnic relations, etc. To some extent, these factors are interrelated, but to a considerable extent they can be considered independent of each other.

Size itself makes a difference in the structure of an area employment complex. The larger a metropolitan area, the more complex is not only its industrial structure, but also its spatial layout of employment and residential areas, its geographical features, its transportation system, its demographic structure, and its institutional structure. Size also encourages higher degrees of specialization in an area's industrial and occupational systems and thus in the degree to which its employment systems are segmented and distinctive.

The result is that each large metropolitan employment complex tends to be unique. Put simply, so many principal variables affect or determine the nature of metropolitan employment complexes that the number of possible combinations of variables is far greater than the number of metropolitan areas. There are, in statistical terms, far more possible cells in the multidimensioned matrix of factors than there are metropolitan areas to fill the cells. One can never be sure what the influence of each of the variables is, in fact. Each metropolitan area, in other words, tends to be unique.

Large metropolitan areas almost inherently have several distinctive components in their industrial base. The largest metropolitan economies in a nation must necessarily be based to a significant degree on activities serving the entire nation and/or one of its major regions. A large metropolitan area must have one or more highly specialized export sectors in which it faces direct competition from only a limited number of other cities. If a city is, in fact, in direct competition with a significant number of other cities in the nation or in its region, there is little reason for any one to be larger than the others.

It takes decades for a large metropolitan area and the city or cities within it to develop. Metropolitan areas which in part serve the entire nation or a major region usually require more than one highly specialized export sector and its related agglomeration if the area is to develop into the size range of 1 million or more workers. Although the American economy is increasingly comprised of service industries, a city and its surrounding metropolitan area almost always must have both a significant service component and a significant manufacturing component if it is to reach the size of 1 million or more. Detroit, based almost solely on automobile manufacturing, and Washington, D.C., based

essentially on the federal government, are the most important exceptions. These exceptions are possible only because automobile manufacturing and the federal government are the largest of all industries in the
country. Even Pittsburgh depends on an agglomeration of steel, machinery, and chemical industries.

Manufacturing industries differ greatly among themselves in their
employment characteristics and thus are a primary force making for
significant differences in employment and labor market processes and
patterns among large metropolitan areas. There are, however, significant differences in other activities which are common to metropolitan
areas, including white-collar work, governmental employment, health,
and educational services and the like.

The metropolitan areas studied here all have agglomerations of both
manufacturing and service activities, in both of which each tends to be
distinctive. New York is based largely on national and international
finance, trade, corporate headquarters, communications, advertising
and related services, and on garment manufacturing. The New York
area is also distinctive for its relatively high proportion of employment
in local government, health, education, and related services. Chicago,
Los Angeles, Houston, and Atlanta are all regional financial, trade,
transportation, and service centers, with varying degrees of national and
international activity. Atlanta is unusually focused on these nodal
activities, but it also has a small aerospace complex and is a state capital.
Chicago is distinctive also for the manufacturing of electrical and other
machinery, steel, printing and publishing, and food products. Los
Angeles is heavily focused on aerospace manufacturing and the fabrication of metals, and Houston on petrochemicals.

The major determinant of employment patterns and processes in a
metropolitan area is its industrial and occupational composition. This
in turn reflects the fact that different industrial and occupational sectors
have different types of employment systems.

While it is common to speak of urban or metropolitan labor markets,
a more useful conception is that of the complex of labor markets and
employment systems which exist in a metropolitan area. Most workers
tend to remain attached to particular employment systems. Only a
relatively small proportion of the workers in a metropolitan area are in
the market at any point in time, actively seeking or open to negotiation
with respect to employment. Only a minority of workers make their way
via markets, i.e., via frequent shifts among jobs or clients, or via
independent professional practice or self-employment.

Most large employers as well as many other sectors of employment
have what might be considered an employment system. One reason for
this is that most large employing organizations seek to have more
control over their manpower needs than a market affords. Large
employers want to have regularized, managed systems to recruit, main-

tain, and develop their own work forces. Another reason is that most workers do not want to be entirely exposed to the vagaries of the market place. They seek via unions, licensing, professional associations, and other devices to control various aspects of recruitment, hiring, training, job tenure, and the like.

Thus, most employment is in the context of an employment system, which is defined by a significant degree of institutionalization and control of the various aspects of the employment relationship. Employer policy, union agreements, government regulation, community groups, and other sources of influence delimit each system by defining particular entry points, by determining the mode of selection of new entrants, the allocation of jobs, promotion routes, and the preparation, eligibility, selection, and training for upward mobility within these systems.

The precise nature of employment systems varies greatly from one industry and occupation to another, for they are heavily influenced by the technology and customs of the industry and occupational field. Thus, recruitment, hiring, promotion, and training processes differ between manufacturing and other industries, between blue-collar, white-collar, professionals, managerial, and other occupational groups. Labor intensive industries tend to have employment systems which differ from those of capital intensive industries. High technology and low technology industries have differing employment systems. Craft unions, particularly in construction, have their own systems controlling hiring, retention, training, etc. Licensed occupations, such as physicians, teachers, nurses, and others help define still other employment systems. Governmental organizations have distinctive employment systems imbedded in civil service systems, collective bargaining, and political practice.

Accordingly, the employment complex of each metropolitan area can best be understood and analyzed with reference to its particular mix of employment systems. The range and relative importance of a metropolitan area's principal industries and sectors will tend to determine not only the nature of its aggregate complex of employment systems, but also, along with its transportation system, the geographical layout of employment centers and residential districts.

Nonmarket institutions play a critical role in the recruitment of workers and in helping workers gain access to employment systems and advancement possibilities. The role of trade unions and professional associations has already been noted. Political organizations play a role not only via patronage, but also in the struggle for power and control by trade unions and professional associations. Political associations may effectively serve as conduits into private employment systems, as in the Chicago area. Public and private schools and employment agencies also serve as conduits into particular employment systems. Access to and movement within employment systems are also influenced by such governmental laws and regulations as civil service, veterans preference, and affirmative action programs. The existence and impact of these governmental programs also depends on political processes which are influenced by associations of employers and employees, community groups, and other political entities. The nature and effect of these nonmarket institutions varies greatly not only from firm to firm, industry to industry, and system to system, but also from metropolitan area to metropolitan area and, indeed, from one part of a metropolitan area to another.

The allocation of different types of jobs among different groups of workers depends in part on the technical requirements of the jobs and the qualities of the workers; in part on the access different groups have to information; in part on how they are perceived and dealt with by personnel specialists, supervisors, and co-workers. In this context, the personnel and industrial relations style of particular employment systems, the quality of intergroup relations, and the aggressiveness of and support for different groups by employer policy, union power, political forces, and governmental programs are important determinants of how employment systems operate. These factors, too, vary greatly among firms, systems, and metropolitan areas. Their cumulative impact is generally distinctive in New York, Chicago, Los Angeles, Atlanta, Houston, and presumably other large metropolitan employment complexes.

Access to employment systems and their attractiveness to different groups of workers are significantly affected by the relationship of employment locations to residential opportunities and transportation possibilities for workers at different levels and with different characteristics. Since the layout of employment locations, residential districts, and transportation systems reflect not only current needs but also past public and private investment decisions, these patterns vary greatly from one metropolitan area to another. Accordingly, access to jobs for different types of workers and the availability of different types of employees for particular employment systems vary greatly within a particular metropolitan system and among metropolitan systems.

In New York, for instance, the mass transit system is a necessary aspect of its three major agglomerations: the Wall Street district, the garment district, and the midtown district. Without mass transit, the necessarily huge numbers of workers could not be brought into or out of these high density (employee/acre) districts. In Chicago, both the transit and highway systems focus on the midtown area, except that transit in from the south is not particularly good. To the south are the great industrial and ethnic enclaves. These closely knit ethnic enclaves are clustered around high wage, high pollution steel, refinery, and related manufacturing, and relatively few workers go in or out.

Los Angeles's highway grid defines its scattered employment centers, its lack of a large central agglomeration, and its low population and employment densities. Houston and Atlanta are defined by their focused and circumferential highway systems, with relatively easy access to and from all areas. Atlanta's new subway system should increase access to midtown and promote a greater central agglomeration.

In Houston, managers can find attractive places to live just outside the downtown area. In New York, the distance some executives have to travel to find a residence and community they consider satisfactory hinders the recruitment and in-transfer of middle level managers. Unskilled workers in New York City depend heavily on the subway, but similar workers in some parts of Los Angeles may find themselves isolated without a car.

Because each metropolitan area is made up in part of a unique set of industries and occupations, its labor markets and its growth patterns are dependent on the vagaries of the particular sectors and the factors which influence their growth, decline, or changes in character. New York, for instance, has been particularly influenced by relocation patterns affecting garment manufacturing, changes in the flow of international trade and finance, and the unionization of public and nonprofit employees; Los Angeles and Atlanta respond to changes in the defense budget as it affects the aerospace industry. Houston's fortunes are tied in complex ways to factors affecting petrochemicals.

The growth rates of large metropolitan employment complexes have a diverse set of impacts on how their labor markets and employment systems operate. Rapidly growing large cities tend to have a broader range of growth sectors; not only the specialized services and manufacturing, but also local manufacturing and services and construction tend to grow. More slowly growing areas tend to have expanding specialized and local service activities, but may be losing manufacturing and some other activities, while construction may be at a slower pace.

Rapidly growing areas tend to attract large numbers of whites and men. Slowly growing areas may lose white males, and such growth in employment as occurs may occur among women and minorities. Although the majority of new employees may be under age thirty, rapidly growing areas may absorb new employees at almost all ages. The influx of women into rapidly growing areas may be strong enough to produce net increases in their numbers who are employed even during their late twenties and early thirties, an age span in which their employment often declines in more slowly growing areas.

In slowly growing areas, most young people will enter local employment systems, but substantial numbers, especially young men, may sooner or later relocate to other areas. Moreover, significant relocation from slowly growing areas may occur even among the middle aged, while retirements may tend to occur earlier than in rapidly growing areas.

Differences in growth rates of metropolitan areas also make for differences in the way in which employment systems operate. Where there are many employment systems which are declining or growing slowly, promotion and advancement possibilities may be limited. This means that these systems are not so attractive to those who ordinarily have the greatest opportunities for upward mobility, i.e., white males. Significant numbers of them may leave, some after high school graduation, some via college or university, and still others in middle age.

In a slow growth situation, the opportunities that come open via retirement or withdrawal of incumbents may tend to be taken by members of minority groups. Those that are attractive despite a lack of growth may be the source of controversy, control, and concealment, as the social groups which are incumbent seek to reserve the posts for their friends, relatives, and others who are socially congenial and acceptable to them. Some of the more complex succession issues occur among the principals of small businesses. Because these opportunities are not a part of formal systems, but rather often depend heavily on informal contact systems for sales, credit, advice, and information, small businesses in which the principals are members of distinctive ethnic groups may simply evaporate as their principals retire or leave for other areas or lines of business. This has apparently been a particular problem in New York City where aging ethnic groups are associated with particular lines of small business; it may be a special problem in the future in Los Angeles, another city distinctive for certain lines of small businesses.

In moderately growing employment systems and complexes, opportunities for advancement are more likely to occur, but they tend to be filled by those who have entered particular systems at an earlier age. When systems and complexes are growing rapidly, there are likely to be many opportunities for people to advance by moving among employment systems. Such rapidly growing systems and complexes may provide employment opportunities in a broad range of occupations for both men and women past fifty and perhaps sixty years of age.

Metropolitan areas tend to differ significantly in the rate at which their young people enter employment as they pass through their teens and reach maturity. This seems to depend on a set of interrelated factors: the industrial and occupational mix of jobs, educational patterns in the area, overall growth rates in the area, opportunities to gain income outside of employment, and perhaps other institutional factors. These forces may have contradictory effects in a particular city. The blue-collar nature of the employment structure in the Chicago and Houston areas tended to be associated with early school-leaving patterns and high labor force participation rates for men of all ages. However, women had low labor force participation rates in Houston, but high rates in Chicago. Despite the heavy concentration of "female" occupations in the New York garment industry, white-collar sector, and hospital, educational, and governmental sectors, New York tended to have low labor force participation rates for women at all ages. This may have reflected both high rates of attendance at high schools, colleges, and graduate schools and the relatively greater availability of welfare and unemployment compensation.

Educational choices tend to be more crucial in more slowly growing areas. This is because most of the new jobs are in the white-collar and professional occupations and competition for the better jobs is more fierce. Also, because upward mobility may be limited in a no-growth local economy, the point of initial entry into the system is a stronger determinant of later experience. Obviously, other factors may be operative. Competition for a wide range of jobs tends to encourage high educational standards in New York, and this is particularly supported by the civil service unions, in part to justify higher salaries. In Chicago, which is also a slow growth area, the political configuration resists higher educational standards in civil service and elsewhere and justifies it on the basis of the blue-collar character of the local population.

While large metropolitan areas attract manpower from throughout the nation and indeed the world, the catchment areas for each metropolis tend to have a unique configuration. The largest cities tend to attract relatively more people from abroad because they have better transportation links to foreign countries, have more international firms and activities, and are better known abroad. Large cities of the second and lower ranks tend to draw relatively more from their adjacent regions. Rapidly growing areas attract younger populations and thus have a higher degree of residential mobility.

The fact that each metropolitan area has a distinctive complex of employment systems does not significantly affect the occupations of those who are employed prior to age eighteen, i.e., prior to high school graduation. Very young workers tend to be employed in substantially the same occupations regardless of the city and its particular employment complex. Young adults are, first of all, sorted out by educational requirements and criteria; as high school graduates and then college and professional school graduates enter the labor force, an increasing differentiation occurs among cities in the employment patterns of their young workers. Since some enter systems with advancement possibilities and others do not, the older the workers, the greater the differentiation among cities.

These patterns apply primarily to men. Men are more likely than women to gain access to the distinctive and preferred employment systems of each city. Thus employment patterns are more similar from city to city for women than for men.

Minority men sometimes gain access to preferred employment systems and sometimes not. This is not simply a North vs. South variable. Each metropolitan area tends to be unique not only in its complex of employment systems, but also in those parts of its complex to which members of minority groups have considerable or limited opportunities. This reflects the complex social structure of each community: the lines of information flow within communities; intergroup attitudes and relationships in general and in particular employment systems, managements, and unions; the precise role played by credentials, tests, and other employment criteria in particular employment systems; and the bargaining with respect to minorities that goes on implicitly or explicitly in local political, union, and industrial relations systems. In any city, there can be startling exceptions to general patterns for minority groups. By implication one can expect significant variation from city to city in the degree to which the majority group dominates or shares the employment within different sectors of the local employment complex. By implication, also, the employment patterns of other ethnic minorities may vary from city to city.

There are a number of other formulations we have not investigated, but which we think may differ significantly in character from one major metropolitan employment complex to another. Preparation for, information about, and access to jobs are likely to be related to where a person's formative years are spent. Accordingly, the ease with which new entrants are absorbed into employment systems may depend on whether their families are located near employment centers or in outlying, essentially residential, areas, and whether they are locals, in-migrants from other areas, or immigrants from abroad. The new generation of young people in the suburbs of New York, for instance, seems more isolated from the principal employment centers of New York than are the young in, say, Los Angeles, Houston, or Atlanta. The proportion of in-migrants is usually high in Houston, while New York has an unusually high proportion of legal and illegal immigrants from distant countries. Houston and Los Angeles gain significant numbers of illegal and legal immigrants, but primarily from nearby parts of Mexico. The character of recruitment and job-finding processes must therefore differ among these as well as among other large metropolitan employment complexes.

In particular, the increasing frequency with which marriages are broken, the increasing informality and variety of types of cohabitation, the increased number of family members who are working (husbands, wives, and others), the increasing emphasis on leisure and retirement, the frequency with which persons change their residence for work related and nonwork related reasons, and the possibility of interrupted and changed careers—all these factors have significant employment effects. There is some evidence that these new patterns are common to all areas, but vary in incidence and intensity among them.

The thrust of the foregoing is that employment is only partially affected by such economic factors as supply, demand, and wage rates. An adequate understanding of each metropolitan employment complex requires a careful integration of these market and nonmarket forces.

CHAPTER
7

Policies and Programs for Large Metropolitan Employment Complexes

This study started with several theses. The first is that there is a tendency in contemporary analyses of urban economies and urban labor markets to search for generalizations based on averages and average relationships with respect to cities and metropolitan areas. Second, as a result, the largest cities and areas are often excluded from analyses because they are "not typical" or because, if given a weight relative to their size, they would "unduly bias" the averages. Sometimes large cities and metropolitan areas are included in analyses, but given the same weight as other smaller cities or metropolitan areas. The result of either excluding large cities or giving them equal weight with much smaller cities is to produce analyses which are more relevant to small and medium sized cities than to large cities and metropolitan areas.

Thirdly, when studies of large cities are made, they are usually focused on a single city. Without some reference point, it is often difficult to identify what is significant or commonplace for that single city. The problem is not fully resolved by bringing together reports by several analysts, even when each uses a more or less common framework to analyze a particular city or metropolitan area; the similarities and differences which emerge may reflect either actual differences among the cities or different points of view or interests of the several analysts.

The primary impetus here to search for a useful, comparative way to analyze large cities and metropolitan areas in terms of their similarities and differences comes from the realization that there is a steady drift in the responsibility for cities and their problems away from local government and to the state and federal governments. To the extent that higher level governments and their programs are developed to fit some conception of the "average" city, they tend to respond more to medium sized cities than to large cities. They tend, moreover, to be more relevant to those cities which somehow are "average." Some cities which do not fit the average may be helped very little by "averaging" policies, while others may be helped very much.

The shift in responsibility from cities to state and federal governments had its origins in the 1930s, if not earlier, but has been accelerating in recent years. The state is, of course, the constitutional father of the city. States have long been concerned with the powers and responsibilities of cities and suburbs. But as the cities have faced increasing troubles with respect to local economic conditions, employment and unemployment, social relations, and fiscal capacity, and as the interrelatedness of city and suburb has become more evident, the federal and state governments have increasingly become the source of funds, program concepts, standards, and assessments for a wide range of local activities.

Whatever the program—public welfare, health services, manpower services, economic development—there has been a continuing dilemma with respect to how federal and local responsibilities will be sorted out and executed. On the one hand, we have the political convention that favors local approaches to local problems. The wisdom of that dogma is supported by the thrust of the present analysis. Each metropolitan area has unique aspects in its industrial, occupational, and demographic structures: its geographical setting and its transportation system linking residential and employment districts; its educational, training, hiring, and promotional complexes and processes; and its business, intergroup, industrial relations, and political styles. The result is that each metropolitan employment complex is in some measure unique in its structure, its institutions, and its employment processes and outcomes. In order to deal effectively with metropolitan employment complexes, each must be approached individually, recognizing and responding to their distinctive qualities.

At the same time, we are a single nation, and Congress legislates with national goals in mind. Congress is expected to deal in an even-handed fashion with respect to different geographic areas. The question raised here is how that evenhandedness is to be achieved in a pluralistic society and economy made up of distinctive metropolitan areas.

One approach is to simply pass funds through to local agencies to be used as they see fit to deal with whatever problems they choose—a kind of simple revenue sharing. The theory in this case is that each local government is best able to define its own needs and wants and is best equipped to allocate its income among various classes of expenditures so as to optimize the community's welfare.

Congress, in allocating monies to local governments, has sought to pursue diverse goals: first, to deal with particular problems which it thinks merit a federal response; second, to respond to the degree of a problem or need as among particular population groups, industries, cities, etc.; third, to insure equity; and, fourth, to promote equality.

BIASES IN FORMULA GRANTS

In its approach to certain problems which it thinks require a federal response and in its desire to respond to the degree of a problem, Congress often uses allocation formulae which contradict the goals of equity and equality. For instance, certain kinds of federal programs are triggered by the percentage of the local labor force or population which is in a certain class, such as being unemployed, on welfare, or in a certain age range. Such trigger devices may work either to the disadvantage or advantage of large metropolitan areas, depending on the circumstances. If the trigger point is less than that which generally prevails in the large cities, large cities will tend on average to get less aid than would a set of small cities with an aggregate characteristic equal to that of the larger cities. The reason is that one could expect, with normal variations, for some smaller cities to be eligible even when the larger city is not eligible. On average, a higher amount of aid thus goes to the set of smaller cities than to larger cities with an equal incidence of the problem.

On the other hard, if the trigger point is greater than that which generally prevails in large cities, the latter will usually be ineligible for aid. However, given any reasonable variation within a set of smaller cities with aggregate populations and problems equal to those of the large city, some of the small cities will not be eligible when the larger city is eligible. On average, a larger amount of aid will tend to go to the larger city than to the set of small cities with equal aggregate incidence of the problem.

The moral of the story is that a trigger formula has a built-in bias against large cities if the trigger point of the formula is less than that which prevails in the general population. However, the trigger point may be biased in favor of large cities if it is set at a level above that which prevails in the society in general.

The position of a particular area with respect to trigger points may change over time. Prior to 1969, for instance, New York City tended to have unemployment rates lower than the rest of the nation, even in recessions, and its concern with unemployment issues was accordingly less. Since 1970, however, New York City has tended to have unemployment rates greater than those of the nation as a whole, and it is as a result increasingly concerned with policies and programs to deal with unemployment. Formerly, New York City was less likely to experience levels of unemployment which produced special efforts in its behalf; now it may get more aid than would a set of smaller cities with equal aggregate employment and unemployment.

FEDERAL POLICIES AND METROPOLITAN GROWTH

The interrelationship between the rate of growth of a metropolitan economy and the nature of its labor market processes and outcomes was noted in Chapter 5. This suggests how fundamentally important it is for the federal government to be evenhanded in the way in which its policies affect the growth, stability, or decline of each city and metropolitan area. This suggests in turn that we need very badly to distinguish for each city and metropolitan area, or at least for the very largest ones, the relative importance of the major forces affecting its size. Each city is a complex local economy. The growth or decline of a city depends in part on whether it is becoming an increasingly better or poorer place to carry on certain lines of business. Thus, a city or a part of its economy grows because it is becoming an increasingly favorable place to carry on certain businesses. Contrariwise, the city or parts of it may fail to grow or may decline because it is no longer a good place to carry on particular lines of business. This can occur either because the nature of those lines of business has changed so that they no longer have growth potential in general or in that particular city, or because congestion, pollution, crime, or high rents or land values make a particular city less attractive for that particular activity.

The point is that particular cities usually grow or decline for fundamental reasons affecting the unique mix of industrial sectors of which they consist. Public policies and the local economic, political, and social climate may contribute to or counteract the effect of these underlying forces, but only in a marginal way.

Intertwined with the above forces making for the growth and decline of local economies are the effects of diverse federal policies which contribute to or inhibit the growth and decline of particular local economies: defense spending patterns, export and import policies, transportation policies, and attendant spending pattern policies, and patterns with respect to the distribution of social security, welfare, health and other transfer payments, taxation policies and the differential effects they may have on different cities, public works programs, environmental programs, etc.

As the preceding analysis suggests, each federal program and policy area, far from being neutral, usually has a differential effect on particular cities.

The problem can be illustrated by noting that the legislative interests of different cities vary greatly. New York City tends to have limited interest in federal highway funds and high interest in federal mass transit funds; Los Angeles has a reverse set of interests. Los Angeles, Atlanta, and Houston are deeply concerned with the letting of aerospace contracts; New York and Chicago have limited interest in these funds. Houston has limited interest in welfare and Medicare programs; New York is deeply interested in these programs. New York has benefited greatly from the rapid inflow of foreign capital in the 1970s, for it has strengthened New York's position as an international financial center. Atlanta has a different interest in the inflow of foreign capital; Atlanta has been a capital-poor area and its banks, real estate entrepreneurs, and others seek foreign funds to meet local needs. Houston, on the other hand, generates great cash flows locally on the basis of its interests in oil and mineral depletion allowances, petrochemicals extraction and manufacturing, and petrochemical and other transportation activities. Houston thus meets an unusually high proportion of its capital needs locally, and exports capital to other cities and countries. It has, therefore, limited interest in federal funds for building its infrastructure of highways, streets, sewers, water mains, etc.

This raises a host of questions for which there are not very clear answers. It is not obvious for any city what the impact has been or will be of the changing advantages and disadvantages it offers to various lines of businesses, including the economies and disadvantages of agglomeration. Nor is it clear what the effects of its own public policies, community attitudes, and other business and trade union policies will be, or how it will be directly and indirectly affected by diverse federal policies.

What are the equities in the allocation of federal funds as among large cities that are undergoing varying rates of growth, with some growing faster than others and still others declining? This study illustrates clearly that the nation is made up of a system of cities. Formerly, cities grew by drawing in rural populations and immigrants. This continued during the postwar years as the suburbs grew from the out-migration from the cities. Although rural to urban migration, immigration, and cities to suburb movements continue, the 1960s clearly represented a period of great movement among metropolitan areas. This is continuing in the 1970s, along with a significant urban to rural movement.

The question raised here is what will be federal policy with respect to the changing balance among the collection of metropolitan areas which largely make up the United States, and particularly among the areas with populations of, say, above 1 million which comprise about 55 percent of the total population. We need to anticipate, rather than perceive after the fact, what impact federal policies will have on the metropolitan character of our nation. It is commonplace now that a considerable part of the central city to suburban relocation of the past 35 years was encouraged by federal policies with respect to low-cost loans for housing, deductibility of property taxes from homeowners' taxable income, and highway construction. Earlier, the growth of cities reflected other federal policies: high tariffs encouraged the growth of manufactures; immigration policies helped provide some of the needed manpower; transportation policies helped create a system to move raw materials and finished goods in and out of large cities; and agriculture policies, particularly federal and federal-state research and information programs and support for the nitrate and other chemical industries, led to agricultural productivity increases which were more rapid than increases in demand and thus to labor displacement in agriculture and farm-to-city migration.

As a general rule, growth situations ought to be self-financing via local taxes and borrowing. That is, a growth situation ought to create jobs, wages and salaries, sales, incomes, land and rental values, and profits, plus taxes on these increases in incomes and values sufficient to underwrite the direct and indirect needs and demands for public services and facilities as a result of the economic and population expansion which is created. Certainly, areas which are losing jobs, income, and population (and their tax base) to the expanding areas ought not to be taxed in order to finance public services and facilities in other competitive areas.

We may have slipped into federal policies which encourage the growth of some metropolitan areas at the expense of other, relatively static or declining areas. A major device is the allocation of grants-in-aid to growing economies and communities on the ground that their growth creates a clearer "need" for new facilities. The "need" may be based simply on added land area and population, on growing congestion and pollution, or simply on rapidly changing tax rates.

One problem is that we do not understand the nature of large urban agglomerations well enough to know whether or not various policies are socially desirable. The accumulation of some activities in one location often creates so-called external economies as well as external diseconomies. The external economies make it more profitable to carry on certain activities in these locations, while the external diseconomies make these or other activities more costly to carry on in that particular location. Depending on the activity, therefore (and as the level and nature of external economies and diseconomies at particular locations change), the location becomes either more or less attractive to diverse activities. Also, land values and rental rates for particular locations respond in part to the changing nature of the demand for those locations. Some kinds of business activities grow at that particular location; others relocate. Sometimes the relocation is merely a rolling shift from the inner to the outer periphery of a particular area; in other cases the relocation may be to another district in the city or metropolitan area; in still other cases, the relocation may be to another region, city, or even country.

The point of all this is to say that it is extremely difficult to unravel, even in retrospect, what has been the effect of a wide range of factors on a local economy. Within this context, it is unusually difficult to pinpoint the effects of increasing or decreasing agglomeration. For that reason, federal policies which contribute to increasing and decreasing agglomeration must be approached with considerable caution. Once underway, the destruction of external economies or the creation of undue external diseconomies can create pressures for relocation which become cumulative. As an agglomeration loses its *raison d'etre*, there can be a continued destruction of values in land, buildings, organizations, and other social investments. This problem is particularly significant for large metropolitan areas for they consist of unique sets of interrelated, interdependent agglomerations.

The question of whether national policy ought to utilize national revenues to help some metropolitan areas grow at the expense of the decline of others is quite separate from the question of whether national policy ought to be neutral, supportive, or negative with respect to the growth and decline of particular metropolitan areas or those of particular size classes. Some have argued that our largest cities and metropolitan areas have become so large as to be inefficient or unlivable. Others have long argued that urban life creates more advantages than disadvantages—more efficiencies than inefficiencies—as compared to rural life, and that the increasing urbanization of the American population was on balance good. Still others have supported policies to protect and encourage rural life and relocation to nonmetropolitan areas. We do not think economic theory offers any significant insight to support or reject ideas to limit the size of metropolitan areas, to establish model or satellite cities, or to promote a return to the land. Values are more important than efficiency in dealing with these issues.

MANPOWER POLICIES AND PROGRAMS

This analysis suggests that each city and metropolitan area requires a somewhat different set of manpower and employment programs tailored to the character of local employment opportunities and needs. These programs should reflect the local industrial and occupational structure, expected growth patterns, the extent to which employment opportunities providing upward or lateral mobility can be expected to appear, and the opening of opportunities in particular industries and occupations because incumbent workers will be promoted, leave for other fields, withdraw from the labor force, or die.

Localized planning and programs are, of course, a basic thrust of the Comprehensive Employment and Training Act. The present analysis emphasizes strongly the wisdom of localized approaches. It also reveals the nature of the similarities and differences among large metropolitan employment complexes and therefore the range of local particularities to which planners must respond. This analysis emphasizes the special attention which local plans will have to give, not only to industrial and occupational patterns, but also to differences in growth rates, demographic structures, and transportation systems linking employment and residential locations. Even more important, this analysis has emphasized that there are crucial differences among labor markets in how recruiting, hiring, training, and promotion systems work, and in the quality and effect of union-management agreements, industrial relations in general, intergroup relationships, and the impact of political groups and political style on the labor market.

This analysis also suggests that political and manpower officials need to keep alert to the probable death rates for different kinds of firms in each community and the implications this has for different groups of workers. As noted earlier, something like a survival contest often occurs in a particular community between companies and workers. In some cases, a company dies (or moves) at a time when it has large numbers of relatively old workers, in their fifties or sixties, who have few prospects for reemployment. In other cases, the company outlives its older workers; i.e., they retire and are replaced by new, young workers. Later, the company may expire or relocate, leaving the new workers stranded. The workers are likely to differ greatly in the two types of cases, not only in age, but also by race or ethnic group, responsibilities, and opportunities. They also present somewhat different problems in tems of public programs for income support, training, reemployment, relocation, etc.

In many cases, however, the expiration of older firms and the withdrawal of older entrepreneurs and workers create opportunities for new groups. This is particularly true in small business. Replacement opportunities are likely to be greater in New York than in most cities, both because of the large numbers of older entrepreneurs and businesses in it and because its business system has an unusually high proportion of small firms. Financial, training, and other programs to aid small businessmen, especially minority businessmen, should be given special emphasis in the New York area. There have been and will continue to be many opportunities for small business in areas like Atlanta and Houston, but of a somewhat different character than in New York. Sheer growth in Atlanta and Houston creates a broad range of opportunities for small businesses in retailing, service, construction, trucking, etc.

The fact that manpower and other programs should be tailored to meet local situations does not necessarily mean that decisions must be left entirely to local political, industrial and other officials. Local problems may require outside influence and guidance if they are to be dealt with effectively.

While federal and federally supported policies and programs should be responsive to the distinctive structures and institutions of particular metropolitan economies and employment complexes, this does not necessarily mean that they should be locally determined and controlled. Rather, inequality, inequity, and other problems are the direct result of local structures and institutions. Federal policies and programs should be tailored to overcome these local forces if it is to achieve its goals. The issue then becomes, for example, how shall federal officials deal with the unusually rigid civil service rules in the New York area? How shall federal officials deal with the political structure in Chicago which seeks to convert each federal program to its own ends? This may involve overriding the local political forces, it may involve creating sets of incentives and penalties making the national goals attractive or acceptable to local political forces, or some combination of the two. This is in essence accomplished by regulations, laws, penalties, withholding of funds, publicity, and a host of other devices.

Federal leverage could also be useful to activate entrenched bureaucracies which are not responsive to changing labor market realities. The evidence is strong, for instance, that the educational system in New York City is increasingly out of touch with many neighborhood communities and with the manpower needs of the local economy. The many reasons for this double estrangement are by no means confined to the usual scapegoats. Without assigning blame, it is nevertheless clear that the system is in trouble and therefore might well benefit from outside pressures which might introduce new possibilities to the resolution of its fiscal, organizational, political, and social problems.

EDUCATIONAL POLICIES

This study raises a number of questions about the relationship between the nature of educational and training programs in different metropolitan areas. There clearly is a relationship between local economies and their educational programs. Students tend to remain in school longer, and more of them complete high school and college in an advanced service and white-collar center with a shrinking manufacturing base like New York than is true in metropolitan areas which are more blue-collar-oriented like Chicago or Houston. Contrary to simple formulations about the connection between education and economic growth, slowly growing areas like New York tend to require or demand higher educational standards than do rapidly growing areas like Houston. Such rapid growth areas provide employment opportunities for local manpower groups which are not highly educated and also depend heavily on in-migrants from other areas, both poorly and highly educated. Clearly, important local political issues in rapidly growing areas turn on the question of the extent to which programs of professional and occupational education should be developed for local population groups vs. how much the local economy shall rely on physicians, engineers, accountants, secretaries, and others who migrate into the growth areas after being trained elsewhere.

Should areas that are losing manpower have a different set of educational and training programs than those that are gaining manpower? The usual pattern is for local authorities to respond to several sets of considerations. First, depressed areas faced with fiscal problems and a lack of new jobs might well limit the scale of local occupational programs which they provide. However, high unemployment tends to encourage young people to stay in school longer simply because they have few alternatives. Young people also demand more education, especially occupational education, because it may help them to get a job when the competition for jobs is strong. Indeed, communities in a no-growth situation may provide educational and training programs for their young residents with the clear expectation that many or most of the graduates will eventually leave.

Education and training in no-growth metropolitan areas thus often provide skills which benefit current residents who are ultimately employed in another metropolitan area, to the benefit of the growing area. With mixed incentives, however, local authorities in no-growth areas probably tend to limit the size and character of such programs to a less than optimum level from the point of view of both the local residents who ultimately move and those who stay and, therefore, from the point of view of the national economy and each of its metropolitan economies.

This argument suggests that Congress, the United States Office of Education, and local educational authorities ought to consider more explicitly the question of desirable education, training, and manpower programs in growth and no-growth areas. In particular, the national interest in financing these programs in no-growth areas ought to be reconsidered. The implication of the above argument is that metropolitan areas which are or can be expected to lose educated and trained manpower should be reimbursed, at least partially, for the extra expense of educating and training those manpower groups. Reimbursement will act both as an incentive to provide education and training opportunities which are not in the narrow interests of the local economy and polity and also to recompense the local system for the investments which it loses as a result of out-mobility.

Growing metropolitan areas should bear all or nearly all the costs of vocationally oriented high school and college programs, for the large majority of local graduates will presumably find local employment. It is extremely doubtful that vocationally oriented programs in growing areas should try to match emerging demand for each type of manpower.

Rather, trained in-migrants from other areas will usually provide a major share of the needs for trained manpower.

LOCAL EMPLOYMENT AND GUIDANCE SERVICES

The nature of information and job-finding assistance which can be feasibly offered to job-seekers is likely to vary from one large metropolitan area to another. However, the larger the metropolitan area, the richer the variety of employment opportunities is likely to be. On the other hand, the larger the city, the more obscure large parts of the local community structure are likely to be to many individuals. In a large city some will be well-informed and have easy access to preferred jobs; others will not. This suggests the need to develop appropriate information and guidance materials for the many different population groups in each large metropolitan area. Such materials would have to be sensitive to the local industrial and occupational structure, as well as alert to the impact of local attitudes, political influences, and other formal and informal institutional patterns unique to the locality.

Attempts to assist in job-finding should also be sensitive to variation in the rate of growth of local employment systems. Stable or no-growth employment complexes are likely to be better known to the local population and, on that account, may require less attention by employment services. Older workers who lose their jobs may be especially hard to place. Moreover, control of entry may be more strongly in the hands of established ethnic and sex groups. The problem of breaking barriers to new ethnic and sex groups may be more difficult in general, although it may be easier in selective situations. The problem of appropriate education and guidance for the young and middle-aged persons who are likely to leave slowly growing employment complexes has already been noted.

Job-finding and placement problems are likely to be quite different in rapidly growing employment complexes. Larger numbers of young and middle-aged persons flowing into the area may not be very well-informed with respect to the nuances and quality of local employment opportunities. Indeed, in a rapidly growing situation, locals may not be very well-informed about new employment systems and opportunities. On the other hand, rapid growth means jobs are available. Moreover, opportunities to advance within particular employment systems or by changing jobs are more plentiful; the quality of information is not likely to be as crucial a determinant of the quality of jobs which are found. Institutional barriers, whether formal or informal, are less rigid and constantly shifting in a rapid growth situation. Even the middle aged find it much easier to locate new jobs in a rapid growth situation. Since the need for information and the availability of opportunity are complexly related to slow and rapid growth situations, the necessary character of guidance and employment services will vary greatly among metropolitan complexes.

The need for timely intermetropolitan flows of information is particularly pointed up by the evidence of growth and decline in the several large metropolitan employment complexes. The relatively abrupt and differential shifts in employment opportunities in the New York and Los Angeles areas and in several of their key sectors is a case in point. Should the growth rates of Houston and Atlanta sharply and unexpectedly change, accurate, differentiated information would be significant for both young and middle-aged persons in many other metropolitan areas.

The spread of metropolitan areas raises questions about how suburban youngsters may relate to central city employment opportunities. The children of those who live and work in the suburbs have some minimum familiarity with the employment systems in and near where their parents work. The children of commuters probably tend to be ill-informed about employment opportunities in both suburbs and cities. This may clearly present significant problems which may increase in the years ahead. On the other hand, young people, particularly those with college and graduate degrees, often do not follow their parents' leads. The implication is that college and university placement systems and employment services may play an increasing role in finding jobs for young people from suburbia, whether in their home suburbs, elsewhere in their home metropolitan areas, or into new metropolitan areas. The need for college placement services will be particularly strong in areas like New York which have high college attendance rates and are also both attracting and losing large numbers of educated young people.

MOBILITY PROBLEMS

This analysis suggests that the debate over whether jobs for the unemployed should be created in the private or the public sector does not fully face the issue. Nor does the debate over whether manpower training should be provided on-the-job or in institutions seem particularly apposite. Rather, the important question is whether the unemployed and manpower trainees will gain access to employment systems which will help them to regularize their employment and provide them with opportunities and mechanisms for upward mobility. The kinds of training and entry jobs which provide such regularity and mobility will depend on the industrial and occupational structure of each city. The problems which must be dealt with to provide entry to favorable employment systems will depend on the local formal and informal control systems and other institutional forces which will vary from field to field and city to city.

The country is entering a period during which, for both demographic and economic reasons, the total labor force and employment may not grow as fast as during the last two decades. If so, growth of the major metropolitan areas will be more limited than it was in the 1960s. Occupational mobility will also be more limited. This will mean that occupational preparation and initial entry into particular employment systems will continue to be a highly important determinant of subsequent employment experience. The conflict for good jobs promises to be a major issue until the rate of employment growth significantly accelerates or until we enter a period of slow growth in the labor force late in the 1980s.

Large metropolitan areas face special problems in maintaining an attractive urban milieu in order to attract and retain key manpower groups which have good opportunities in other locations. This is an issue for managerial personnel, academics, physicians, and other professionals—indeed for those in any occupation with a regional, national, or international labor market. Public service employment to provide cleaner, better maintained streets, sidewalks, parks, and vacant lots, as well as personal security, might be particularly significant in New York and perhaps Chicago, which have special needs to be attractive to footloose businesses, corporate headquarters, international business activities, business visitors, tourists, conventioneers, and the like. However, it may be quite difficult to use public service employment programs for these tasks in New York because public employee unions will insist strongly on maintaining their wage and working standards.

PUBLIC SERVICE JOBS

The character of public employment programs might be different in different places for other reasons. For instance, efforts to convert welfare expenditures into jobs can have a greater impact on New York, say, than Houston, simply because there are relatively more people on welfare in the former than the latter. Public works programs to rehabilitate housing may be relatively larger in New York and Chicago simply because they have so many more older residences relative to their population.

One must also note that some public bureaucracies, such as New York's, have been unusually apt in the past in undertaking new federal programs and have created more local jobs thereby. This tendency may be somewhat less strong in the future, for New Yorkers have grown somewhat more cautious with respect to the full fiscal implications of new programs. However, New York will probably still utilize new programs to a greater extent than Chicago or Houston. One can probably expect the Chicago authorities to spend considerable time working out the power and patronage implications of any new federal programs before they undertake them. The Houston political system will undoubtedly continue to have limited interests in new federal programs.

WELFARE REFORM

On the other hand, federal policies to rationalize and equalize welfare standards and payments would have a significantly different impact on different cities. In Houston, for instance, the number receiving welfare payments and the level of payments per person might tend to increase dramatically, and might significantly reduce labor force participation rates there among those with marginal attachments to employment. On the other hand, federalization might mean lower federal payments per person in New York, unless supplemented by special state and/or local payments, and thus might force significant numbers of the mothers of young children onto the labor market.

RESEARCH NEEDS

The point of view consistently taken here is that each metropolitan area is differentiated from every other area to a significant degree. At the same time, the influence of the federal government continues to grow, especially as the country is shifting from external concerns of defense and space and emphasizing internal programs to improve conditions in the diverse populations. Common goals do not require identical programs. On the contrary, a pluralistic economy and society requires different policies and programs in different situations in order to achieve common goals. Diversity is an appropriate social goal; it should be encouraged rather than constrained.

The preceding analysis reveals not only the necessity to consider each large metropolitan area as an integrated complex of structural and institutional attributes, some of which are distinctive to that area. It also reveals that our understanding of large metropolitan employment complexes falls far short in many ways of our needs if we are to develop effective policies and programs.

We need to develop better data and models for the projection of the changing character of large metropolitan employment complexes. As the earlier chapters make clear, particularly Chapters 1 and 2, each metropolitan area contains a complex of employment markets and systems. The boundaries of a metropolitan area are not necessarily significant for particular employment markets or systems. Labor markets may be viewed from the point of view of either individual workers or individual employers. From either point of view the labor markets may be aggregated along conventional segmentation lines: industrial, occupational, demographic, and the like. A labor market includes not only those who are employed in it, but also those who might be attracted into it. In geographical terms, a particular labor market may be largely confined to a particular neighborhood or district in a city, suburb, or metropolitan area; it may extend to the whole city or metropolitan area, or it may extend to the region, nation, or other parts of the world. We need considerably more conceptualization and research into how to collect data from individuals and enterprises which would permit us to define labor markets which are relevant to individuals, enterprises, and groups of each. Manpower programs, for instance, need data collected so as to accurately reflect the opportunities of their potential clients. Equal employment programs which seek to relate the employment patterns of employees to the availability of minority and women workers in particular labor markets often do not have adequate data on what labor markets are relevant for particular employers or for particular kinds of workers.

We need data and models for individual metropolitan areas—both in their parts and entirety—but we also need the capacity to analyze them as a system of metropolitan areas. We need to know how employment in particular areas relates in industrial, occupational, and demographic terms to national trends, as well as how competing and complementary metropolitan areas relate to each other. We also need a better understanding of the changing advantages and disadvantages each metropolitan area offers to particular industrial sectors. This includes a better understanding of the changing economics of particular enterprises within industries, including the aging and obsolescence of their entrepreneurs, work force, and capital equipment and other factors which are relevant to their expansion, contraction, expiration, or relocation. We also very badly need studies to assess the impact on particular metropolitan areas of particular programs to deal with macroeconomic problems. That is, we need to understand the implications for different metropolitan areas of investment tax credits; interest rate changes; defense spending; welfare programs; public employment programs; programs to build or rebuild particular parts of the infrastructure; foreign trade policies, etc.

We also need considerably more research into the economic, social, and political forces affecting the institutions which determine the allocation of jobs among different ethnic, racial, religious, and sex groups in different metropolitan areas. The quite different way in which the political systems of the five cities studies here operate via patronage, testing mechanisms, affirmative action programs, and public and private bargaining points to a badly needed reassessment of these phenomena in different metropolitan settings.

This study also questions certain conventional assumptions about investment in human resources and economic development. Metropolitan areas with high per student investment may be the most slowly growing, while rapidly growing areas rely heavily on the in-migration of manpower groups with skills developed elsewhere. If these questions were explored within the context of several metropolitan areas the complex nature of the relationship between education, individual advancement, and economic growth could be much better illuminated. A careful reevaluation of the role educational policies and programs play in different metropolitan areas would thus pay attention to a number of variables: whether the area was growing or not; the current and changing industrial, occupational, and demographic character of the area; in-migration and out-migration of different groups defined by sex, race, ethnic group, education, and occupation; and the way in which different local employment systems operate to attract, reject, and retain different groups.

The efficiency of local and national labor markets depends heavily on the quality of the information available. This is true in general, but particularly true where groups such as minorities and women are entering fields where they are underrepresented. We have some evidence that the quality of the information available as well as the mix of institutions providing information is different in different metropolitan areas.

The question of how information about and access to employment is gained in different metropolitan areas therefore needs to be explored from a number of points of view. One approach would be via different population groups: new graduates of educational institutions; city dwellers and suburbanites; young and middle-aged men and women; locals and in-migrants; different ethnic, racial, and language groups, etc. Another approach would be via different kinds of employment systems: civil service; large and small businesses; highly technical and low-skilled occupations; union organized and market oriented systems, etc. A third approach would be to study the role of different intermediaries in different locations: guidance and placement officers in schools and colleges; want ads; public and private employment services; informal contacts, etc.

There need to be more studies of the structure of local labor markets. The several studies in the Chicago area of the structure of wage rates, industrial and ethnic enclaves, and the role of the transportation system are suggestive of studies that might be undertaken in other metropolitan areas. In each area, moreover, we need more careful attention to the strata which exist within what are often treated as single occupations or occupational groups. For example, there are differences in each metropolitan area between general, legal, accounting, and financial secretaries and clerical workers which have not been well studied. Moreover, different areas have different degrees of specialization in these and other suboccupations, in part due to differences in the size of metropolitan area. We do not know very much about career systems and mobility patterns within and among the several specialized secretarial and clerical suboccupations. Better knowledge of these patterns would be useful not only to the workers in these fields, but also to guidance and employment specialists who advise potential workers in these fields.

The nature of the competition between employment systems which are distinctive or unusually large in particular metropolitan employment complexes, as well as between them and the more ubiquitous employment systems present in each area, needs to be studied. For instance, what is the relationship between the garment industry and the hospital system in New York, say, in the competition for Puerto Rican women and men? What impact does the presence of the state government in Atlanta have on the labor market for clerical workers in downtown offices? Does the labor market for truck drivers have a different character in, say, Chicago and Houston, where there is a large demand for factory workers, than in Atlanta, where there are relatively few factory workers?

Finally, each large metropolitan area needs to be carefully examined to identify both its common and its distinctive sources of employment disadvantage for women and minorities. A better understanding of the precise nature of difficulties which flow from local educational systems, employment systems, housing, transportation, political processes, and other institutions could be the basis for formulating increasingly precise and effective strategies to achieve equality in each metropolitan area.

This list of research needs is consistent with the central message of this book. We need to appreciate both the common elements and the distinctive qualities of our large urban agglomerations, for such a high proportion of our population lives and works with them. We need to develop policies, administrative structures, and programs which are sensitive to the differences among areas, rather than force our society to adjust to uniformity.

Bibliography

"A Symposium: Equal Employment Opportunity: Comparative Community Experience." *Industrial Relations: A Journal of Economy and Society,* vol. 9, no. 3, May 1970, pp. 277-355.

Abler, Ronald, and John S. Adams, *A Comparative Atlas of America's Great Cities: Twenty Metropolitan Regions.* Minneapolis: University of Minnesota Press, 1976.

Aronson, Robert L., ed. *The Localization of Federal Manpower Planning.* Ithaca: Cornell University, New York State School of Industrial and Labor Relations, 1973.

Atlanta Chamber of Commerce. *Atlanta: Income by Census Tracts.* 1973.

———. *Atlanta: Larger Employers.* 1973.

———. *Atlanta: Market Characteristics of the Black Population.* 1973.

———. *Atlanta Operations of the Fortune 500 Industrial Firms.* May 1972.

———. *Atlanta: Transportation.* 1973.

———. *1972 Metropolitan Atlanta Directory of Manufacturers.* 1972.

Banfield, Edward C. *The Unheavenly City.* Boston: Little Brown & Company, 1968.

Bergman, Barbara R., and Jerolyn R. Lyle. "The Occupational Standing of Negroes by Areas and Industries." *The Journal of Human Resources.* 6:4, Fall 1971, pp. 411-33.

Berry, Brian, with Peter G. Goheen and Harold Goldstein. *Metropolitan Area Area Definition: A Re-Evaluation of Concept and Statistical Practice.* Washington: Department of Commerce, Bureau of the Census. Working Paper no. 28, 1968.

Brecher, Charles. *Upgrading Blue Collar and Service Workers.* Baltimore: The Johns Hopkins University Press, 1972.

Briggs, Vernon M., Jr. *The Houston Labor Market.* Washington: U.S. Department of Labor, Manpower Administration, Manpower Research Monograph no. 23. Negro Employment in the South. vol. I, 1971.

Bullock, Paul. *Youth in the Labor Market: Employment Patterns and Career Aspirations in Watts and East Los Angeles.* Institute of Industrial Relations. Los Angeles: University of California, January 1972.

Camil Associates. *Recruitment, Job Search and the U.S. Employment Service.* Philadelphia, 1975.

Chinitz, Benjamin. *City and Suburb: The Economics of Metropolitan Growth.* Englewood, N.J.: Prentice-Hall, 1964.

Conservation of Human Resources. *An Economic Development Agenda for New York.* New York: Columbia University, 1975.

———. *The Corporate Headquarters Complex in New York City.* New York: Columbia University, 1977.

Dahl, Robert. *Who Governs?—Democracy and Power in an American City.* New Haven: Yale University Press, 1961.

deTorres, Juan. *Economic Dimensions of Major Metropolitan Areas: Population, Housing, Employment, and Income.* New York: National Industrial Conference Board, Technical Paper no. 18, 1968.

Doeringer, Peter B., and Michael J. Piore. *Internal Labor Markets.* Lexington: D. C. Heath, 1971.

Duncan, Otis Dudley, et al. *Metropolis and Region.* Resources for the Future. Baltimore: The Johns Hopkins University Press, 1960.

First National City Bank. *Profile of a City.* New York: McGraw-Hill, 1972.

Freedman, Marcia, with Gretchen Maclachlan. *Labor Markets: Segments and Shelters.* Montclair, N.J.: Allanheld, Osmun & Co., 1976.

———. assisted by Gretchen Maclachlan. *The Process of Work Establishment.* New York: Columbia University Press, 1969.

Friedlander, Stanley. *Unemployment in the Urban Core: An Analysis of Thirty Cities with Policy Recommendations.* New York: Praeger, 1972.

Ginzberg, Eli. *Career Guidance: Who Needs It, Who Provides It, Who Can Improve It.* New York: McGraw-Hill, 1971.

———, ed. *The Future of the Metropolis: People, Jobs, Income.* Salt Lake City: Olympus, 1974.

———. *The Human Economy.* New York: McGraw-Hill, 1976.

———, et al. *New York Is Very Much Alive.* New York: McGraw-Hill, 1973.

Glazer, Nathan. "Social and Political Aging in New York." *Society.* May/June 1976, pp. 45–47.

Gorham, William, and Nathan Glazer, eds. *The Urban Predicament.* Washington: The Urban Institute, 1976.

Granovetter, Mark S. *Getting a Job: A Study of Contacts and Careers.* Cambridge: Harvard University Press, 1974.

Grebler, Leo, Joan W. Moore, and Ralph C. Guzman. *The Mexican American People: The nation's second largest minority.* New York: The Free Press, 1970.

Handlin, Oscar. *The Newcomers: Negroes and Puerto Ricans in a Changing Metropolis.* Cambridge: Harvard University Press, 1959.

Hansen, Niles M. "Urban and Regional Dimensions of Manpower Policy." Prepared for U.S. Department of Labor, Manpower Administration. mimeo. University of Kentucky, June 1969.

Hefner, James A. *Adjustment Patterns of Black and White Migrants in a Southern Labor Market*. Atlanta: Clark College, The Southern Center for the Study of Public Policy, 1973.

―――― and Alice E. Kidder. "Racial Integration in Southern Management Positions," *Phylon*. vol. XXXIII, Summer 1972, pp. 193-200.

Hiestand, Dale L. *Discrimination in Employment: An Appraisal of the Research*. Policy Papers in Human Resources and Industrial Relations 16, Ann Arbor: Institute of Labor and Industrial Relations. University of Michigan—Wayne State University, 1970.

――――. *Economic Growth and Employment Opportunities for Minorities*. New York: Columbia University Press, 1964.

Hoover, Edgar M., and Raymond Vernon. *Anatomy of a Metropolis*. Cambridge: Harvard University Press, 1959.

Johnson, Miriam, and John Walsh. *Help Wanted: Case Studies of Classified Ads*. Salt Lake City: Olympus, 1976.

Knight, Richard V. *Employment Expansion and Metropolitan Trade*. New York: Praeger, 1973.

Kornblum, William. *Blue Collar Community*. Chicago: University of Chicago Press, 1974.

Mangum, Garth, and David Snedeker. *Manpower Planning for Local Labor Markets*. Salt Lake City: Olympus, 1974.

――――, and R. Thayne Robson. *Metropolitan Impact of Manpower Programs: A Four City Comparison*. Salt Lake City: Olympus, 1973.

Marshall, F. Ray. *Labor in the South*. Cambridge: Harvard University Press, 1967.

――――. *The Negro and Organized Labor*. New York: Wiley, 1965.

Marshall, F. Ray, and Vernon M. Briggs, Jr. *The Negro and Apprenticeship*. Baltimore: Johns Hopkins Press, 1967.

――――. *Equal Apprenticeship Opportunities: The Nature of the Issue and the New York Experience*. Ann Arbor: Institute of Labor and Industrial Relations. University of Michigan-Wayne State University, 1968.

Mayer, Harold M., and Richard C. Wade. *Chicago: Growth of a Metropolis*. Chicago: University of Chicago Press, 1969.

Meyer, John, John Kain, and Martin Wohl. *The Urban Transportation Problem*. Cambridge: Harvard University Press, 1965.

Mills, Edwin S. *Studies in the Structure of the Urban Economy*. Baltimore: The Johns Hopkins University Press, Resources for the Future, 1972.

O'Connor, Len. *Clout: Mayor Daley and His City*. New York: Hearst-Avon, 1975.

Palmer, Gladys L. *Labor Mobility in Six Cities: A Report on the Survey of Patterns and Factors in Labor Mobility, 1940–50*. New York: Social Science Research Council, 1954.

Rees, Albert, and George P. Shultz. *Workers and Wages in an Urban Labor Market*. Chicago: University of Chicago Press, 1970.

Reynolds, Lloyd G. *The Structure of Labor Markets: Wages and labor mobility in theory and practice*. New York: Harper, 1951.

Rose, Harold M. *The Black Ghetto: A Spatial Behavioral Perspective*. New York: McGraw-Hill, 1971.

Sayre, Wallace S., and Robert Kaufman. *Governing New York City*. New York: Norton, 1965.

Stanback, Thomas Jr., and Richard V. Knight. *The Metropolitan Economy*. New York: Columbia University Press, 1970.

————. *Suburbanization and the City*. Montclair, N.J.: Allanheld, Osmun & Co., 1976.

Tauber, Karl E. "Racial Segregation: The Persisting Dilemma," *The Annals of the American Academy of Political and Social Sciences*, 422. November 1975, pp. 87-96.

The Port Authority of New York and New Jersey. *People and Jobs: A Forecast of Population, Households, Labor Force, and Jobs in the New York—New Jersey—Connecticut Metropolitan Region, 1975-1990*. New York: The Authority, 1974.

Thomlinson, Ralph. *Urban Structure: The Social and Spatial Character of Cities*. New York: Random House, 1969.

Thompson, Wilbur R. *A Preface to Urban Economics*. Baltimore: The Johns Hopkins University Press, Resources for the Future, 1965.

Twentieth Century Fund Task Force on Prospects and Priorities of New York City. *A Nice Place to Live*. New York: The Fund, 1973.

U.S. Department of Commerce, Bureau of the Census. *Characteristics of the South and East Los Angeles Area*. Current Population Reports, Technical Studies. Series P-23, no. 18. June 28, 1966.

U.S. Department of Labor, Bureau of Labor Statistics, "Employment Situation in Poverty Areas of Six Cities, July 1968-June 1969." *Urban Employment Survey*. BLS Report no. 370. October 1969.

Index

135

ABOUT THE AUTHORS

Dale L. Hiestand is Senior Research Associate, Conservation of
Human Resources Project, Columbia University, and Professor of
Business at Columbia's Graduate School of Business. He is co-
author of *An Economic Development Agenda for New York City*
and has contributed chapters to studies on manpwer, minority
employment problems, and urban economics. Dean W. Morse,
Senior Research Associate, Conservation of Human Resources,
and Adjunct Professor of Economics at Fordham University, is the
author of *The Peripheral Worker* and co-author of *The Labor
Market: An Information System.*